Mystery & Mayhem in Darkest Lincolnshire

Adrian Gray

Bookworm of Retford

Copies of this book are available from
Bookworm, The Retford Bookshop, 01777 869224
and from most high street and online bookshops

Overseas enquiries can be made to
sales@bookwormretford.co.uk

First published 2017
Bookworm of Retford
1 Spa Lane, Retford Notts. DN22 6EA
www.bookwormretford.co.uk

Cover Illustration by Jo Galtry and Burgess Design and Print.
Designed by www.burgessdesignandprint.com, Retford.

ISBN 978-0-9927857-9-6

Copyright Adrian Gray 2017
All rights reserved. No part of this book may be re-printed or reproduced in any form without prior consent in writing from the publisher or author. Any person who does any unauthorised act in relation to this publication may be liable to criminal prosecution and civil claims for damages.

This book is sold subject to the condition that it shall not by way of trade or otherwise, be lent, resold or otherwise circulated without the publisher's prior consent in any form of binding or cover other than that in which it is published and without a similar condition being imposed on the subsequent purchaser.

A catalogue record of this book is available from the British Library.

Contents

1. The King who was killed by a dead man….possibly — 5
2. The Gosherd of Crowland and the Ghost — 11
3. Tales of the Poachers — 16
4. Satan's Cunning Plan — 22
5. Death in the Wash — 29
6. Captain Spitfire — 35
7. The Maddening Member for Lincoln — 43
8. Love, Death and a Maiden — 49
9. The Man who fought against the Darkness — 56
10. The Invasion of Barton — 65
11. Love, the Devil and Redemption in Old Fenland Times — 72
12. The Dark Arts of the Decoy Men — 79
13. Escape from Lincoln Gaol — 84
14. Murder of a King? — 88
15. Canute and the Aegir — 95
16. The Tap at the Window and the Knock at the Door — 101

An Introduction
by Adrian Gray

For a few years I have often travelled down to London for work and found it still to be the case that very few people there really know much about Lincolnshire. However, I got to know two other natives of the county working down there, one of whom commented about returning to 'darkest Lincolnshire' for the weekend. This sparked a thought, because as far as understanding goes it still is a 'dark' place to many from other parts of the country. Others have typically distorted impressions: of course there are many who falsely assume all of Lincolnshire is 'flat'[1] but I was amused by recent visitors from Northern Ireland who declared themselves pleased to be visiting 'the land of sausages'. Indeed, traditional Lincolnshire folk have many uses for a pig.

The stories in this book explore the various meanings of 'darkest' that one might imagine, although none really get close to the type of darkness in Joseph Conrad's *Heart of Darkness*. There is darkness in terms of dark deeds, darkness in terms of dark times, and darkness in terms of ignorance, plus one or two 'things that go bump in the night'. But what I have most wanted to do is to shine some light onto stories of the county that may have been partly or wholly lost in darkness – forgotten or unknown by those who live in Lincolnshire today. Some of these stories are true, some might have been true and some probably never were true. But they are all stories connected with Lincolnshire and so they are worthy of the retelling.

---

[1] Cambridgeshire, Norfolk and Suffolk are all much flatter overall, whilst my favourite 'fact' to challenge this view is that the highest point on the railway between London and Edinburgh is in Lincolnshire.

Chapter One

The King who was killed by a dead man… possibly

'Winter is coming,' the old Saxon bards used to declaim, 'and with it come the Norsemen to steal our cattle and kidnap our children.' All the children knew that the worst of all was Sweyn Forkbeard, the ruthless king from over the cold northern sea.

Sweyn struck terror into the hearts and minds of all who lived in Lindsey – the northern part of what is now Lincolnshire – in the dark days a few years into the second millennium after Christ. Weak King Ethelred could offer little protection when the Danish king sailed his proud longboats up through the mouth of the Humber and then into the Trent, which became his winter home.

Vikings often sailed up the River Trent to Gainsborough and, sometimes, as far as Derby.

Sweyn's vicious behaviour made enemies of the English people, who fought back where they could and one terrible Sunday massacred many Danish settlers, but his own systematic attacks on the treasure houses of the Christian faith made enemies of those who fought with words and prayers.

As his men ranged far and wide by land and water, they brought their own brand of terror into the eastern lands once ruled by the martyred English king, Edmund. The saintly Edmund had been shot and beheaded about 150 years earlier by another bunch of Danes. But the Danes found out that simply killing a man does not ensure that you have got rid of him, and Edmund staged a number of reappearances. Every year a woman opened his coffin to trim his fingernails, which continued to grow, and he was enshrined in an abbey at the town of Boedricsworth – when eight thieves tried to rob this, they were frozen on the spot.

Sweyn did not read the clues that it would be best to leave Edmund's people and the lands of his abbey alone, and continued to harry both. In 1010 Boedricsworth was plundered and the monk Ailwin, custodian of Edmund's shrine and body, took the martyr's remains to London for safety. Ailwin left the body in St Gregory's Chapel, where many miracles were attributed to it.

Now a saint's body that had miraculous powers was a wonderful commercial proposition in those days and the Bishop of London, who was perhaps not as good a man as he should have been, determined to move Edmund to a place where the Bishop could get more control of it – and the money. When Ailwin was off doing good deeds elsewhere, the Bishop sent a few men to carry the shrine to his chosen spot – except they could not move it. Huff and puff as hard as they might, it remained as immovable as 'a great hill of stone' until Ailwin arrived to drive them off.

The Martyrdom of Edmund, King of the Angles, a later iconic English saint.

In the year 1013 Ailwin's tale has another twist. Lying in his rooms one night he had a vision of the saintly Edmund: 'Go to the Danish king,' Edmund declaimed, 'and tell him to leave my people alone – or face God's judgement.'

Ailwin was terrified. It was clear that Edmund thought it his duty to deliver the message in person to Sweyn, but not even the King of England himself – the hapless Ethelred – could stand up to Sweyn and had fled from his throne. Ailwin hesitated to deliver Edmund's message, but as 1014 dawned Sweyn increased the pressure by demanding extra 'taxes' from the monks.

Sweyn had now declared himself King of England and so, in a way, Gainsborough, where he was often based in the winter, became a sort-of 'capital'.

Months had passed during which the unnerved Ailwin did nothing, then Edmund appeared again – less of a vision and more of a physical presence this time. 'Why have you done nothing?' he demanded with the confidence of one who spends most of his time in Heaven, 'Your duty is to give warning to Sweyn.'

One can only imagine the deep sense of dread that must have filled Ailwin as he began his long journey across the Fens and down the Trent to Gainsborough, where the Danish King was holding court. As he arrived at the Danish camp, he was challenged by the surly guards, who had been drinking all day and saw a dirty and dishevelled Christian monk as the ideal subject of their drunken humour.

'Hey, monk,' one shouted, 'are you looking for Jesus?'

Ailwin prayed for guidance, and decided the straight response was best. 'No, actually I've already found him, but I've been sent to speak to King Sweyn.'

The guards roared with laughter – they had found a real joker to liven up their evening! 'On whose orders?' they asked, 'Did God send you?'

Ailwin shuffled his feet, then tried to look as confident as possible. 'Actually, not directly. I have been sent by Saint Edmund.'

After more hilarious laughter, the guards debated the options and decided the story was so good that King Sweyn actually might quite like to meet the mad monk. They checked him for concealed weapons. It would certainly be more entertaining for Sweyn than listening to the poets trundling out the same old heroic myths and legends every night. So they tied Ailwin's hands up, just in case he wasn't a monk who had gone soft in the head, and pulled him into the hall where Sweyn held court.

By the time Ailwin was hauled into the hall, night had fallen. Much food had been eaten, even more alcohol had been drunk, and ladies whose morals left little room for doubt were winding their way amongst Sweyn's band of vicious warriors looking for some attention. But for these Danes women were a distant second best to the thrill of battle and the camaraderie of men steeped in blood, so tales of boasting and bravery were winning out in the contest for attention.

Sweyn's gaze was soon held by the appearance of a mud-spattered monk being dragged along between two of his best guards. 'What have we here?' he roared. 'Is this the best you can find for entertainment?' Sweyn's men also looked up – here was at least novelty from the usual tedium of epic poems and tawdry women.

'So, monk, who are you?' laughed Sweyn.

(Illustration by Jo Galtrey)

Ailwin had no way out, so, praying to his Saviour under his breath, he again went for the direct approach. 'I am Ailwin, guardian of the tomb of Edmund at Boesdricsworth. He has sent me to tell you – no more taxes, no more raids, and no more violence. If you disobey, you will surely die a humiliating death.'

Everyone expected Sweyn to draw his sword and cut off the monk's head, but instead he sat down and smiled. Such a feeble enemy was not worth a cut of the King's sword – he could be killed later, by women!

Instead, Sweyn sat down, smiling. 'Well,' he said, 'I like a challenge. Here I am with all my chiefs around me – what say we all set out for Boedricsworth tomorrow?' Roars of approval. 'And let's take the monk with us – he can introduce us to Edmund himself!'

After this there was more drinking, a bit of fighting and some mingling with the women, but few noticed that Sweyn himself had become almost silent.

A few men were already dozing with their heads on the tables when Sweyn suddenly rose to his feet, sweat dripping from his brow, and pointed in front – his eyes bulging in terror.

'Help, help, fellow soldiers,' he cried, but although they looked around, they could not see how they were meant to help. 'Can't you see – here is Saint Edmund, coming to kill me.'

Sweyn's men were never scared in battle, indeed wanted only to die in battle, but they were all terrified of ghosts and so not a single one moved to stand beside his King. Only Ailwin, chained to a post in the corner, felt a sudden leaping of his heart.

Sweyn suddenly clutched the side of his stomach. 'I am struck by Saint Edmund….!' he cried, and collapsed into his chair. Only then did his courtiers stir, rushing up and searching the King for a stab wound; yet, try as they might, they could find not a scratch, and instead carried the writhing and screaming Sweyn off to the privacy of his own chambers. There he lay all night, clutching at the spot where he said Edmund had stabbed him – sweating, twisting, and muttering the name of 'Edmund.'

A greyfriar monk.

And so when the morning mists of February 1014 started to clear the next day, lingering around the boats on the Trent downhill from the Danes' encampment, Sweyn lay dead. Ailwin was forgotten as Danish warriors whispered about the disgrace of a bloodthirsty king dying an old woman's death in his bed, but others muttered that Sweyn had become over-mighty and some even thought that he had been poisoned by some of the Danish nobles.

Ailwin slipped way from Gainsborough and made his way back to Boedricsworth, which in time became known as Bury St Edmunds, and where the monks rewrote the tales of the Great Deeds of Saint Edmund. They had no doubts as to how the great Sweyn had died. There must have been great scenes as Sweyn's body was loaded onto a Danish ship at Gainsborough for the journey to his burial place at York. Then Ethelred staged a return so that, for a time, the Danish grip on the land ebbed like the tide in the Trent. But they would return, with Sweyn's son Cnut who, as we shall see in another story, wisely made his peace with Edmund's God.

For some chroniclers, the death of Sweyn marked a point when years of darkness and fear started to turn into hope for a better land.

Author's Notes:
This story might be true, or parts of it might be true, or possibly almost none of it is true, but certainly elements of it have been told for a long time. Sweyn (or Swein) died in Gainsborough on 3 February 1014, but as to the rest..... Many anti-Danish sources paint Sweyn as pagan, but there is some evidence that he followed a moderately Christian line and built a couple of churches in Denmark. Ailwin features in the version told in White's History, Gazetteer and Directory of Suffolk when it was printed in 1855. Before that, John Lydgate wrote an account of miracles connected to Edmund during the reign of Henry VI which was based on successive medieval accounts. Florence of Worcester's account tells of Sweyn being struck down by Edmund just after planning a raid on his shrine, whilst John of Tinmouth said that Edmund's ghost stabbed him as he sat in a chair. William of Malmesbury said that he was struck down in his sleep for 'answering rudely' back to Edmund! The most likely explanation is that Sweyn was poisoned, but however he died it was certainly a great day in Gainsborough's history!

There is also a tradition that King Alfred held his wedding feast at Gainsborough as his wife, Elswith, was the daughter of Ethelred the Great, a Mercian earl who lived there.

Chapter Two

The Gosherd of Crowland and the Ghost

Many, many years ago, long before the Dutch engineers came and ruined everything, little fenland towns like Crowland were surrounded by – of course – fen. This isolation was what had attracted the saintly hermit Guthlac in the days long before the Normans came. Much of the fen was common and a man could go searching out birds to eat or take his own stock out to graze in summertime. July was a good time when a lad could enjoy his job of looking after sheep or geese with many an opportunity to snatch a doze in the heat of the day.

And so it was that the young gosherd set out from Crowland one hot morning with his gaggle of a dozen or so geese, which he thought quite the noisiest creatures on God's earth. Shushing them along, he wended his way out into the fen so that the old abbey of Croyland – shrine of the legendary Guthlac – was a mere blob on an otherwise unvaried horizon.

The old town of Crowland was famous for its triangular bridge which once had a canopied cross where pilgrims could stop on their way to the abbey.

The gosherd found a nice spot where it was unlikely someone could see him amongst the reeds and lay down, letting the geese get on with their own business.

Well, the gosherd enjoyed a very pleasant sleep in which the most beautiful girl in Crowland, Betty, declared her undying admiration of him and rejected the waking reality, which was that she preferred the blacksmith's boy to a dull gosherd. But suddenly he woke with a start, thinking at first that there must be someone around to steal the geese. Yet it was still an undisturbed, quiet afternoon with the sun just drooping towards the horizon and no sign of Betty at all.

The gosherd got to his feet and rounded up the geese…..nine, ten, eleven…. still eleven. Where was the twelfth, the big old gander that made so much racket? With an awful sinking feeling, he scanned to the west, then to the south, then the east and finally the north. No sign. He scanned all around again, while the other geese muttered around his feet as if nothing had happened.

Now the gosherd knew the old Bible story about leaving the 99 sheep to go looking for the missing hundredth, but he also knew there were risks in that. So he drove the geese before him back to Crowland and locked them up in their pen, hoping that their owner – Black Tom – would not come past to check them yet awhile. Then he scarpered back out into the fen to look for the missing gander – the biggest, noisiest and theoretically least easy to lose.

As the gosherd wandered here, there and everywhere, he went further out into the marshy areas where even in summer a man or boy had to tread warily. Crowland was hardly visible and even the evening bell for the monks could barely be heard. Fearing retribution, he carried on searching in marsh, toft and reeds with no sign of a goose anywhere. He got to hate the wild ducks, who occasionally tricked him by their movements or scared him when they burst out of some reeds just as he was looking in. But now the sun was down, the grey twilight was gathering and a mist was beginning to rise. The gosherd knew that it was only a fool who stayed out in the marshy fen after dark for there were all manner of boggarts and demons ready to lure man or boy to his doom.

Fearing that the dark would soon arrive and drag him down in its clutches, and fearing Black Tom a little less, the gosherd set out back towards the abbey church which he could still just about see in the gathering gloom – rather distant. He was very fearful, and every duck that flew or bittern that boomed seemed to shake him to the very marrow. The twitch of a reed was all it took to make him jump and every time he saw moving water he thought it was the boggarts come to drag him under.

Eventually he arrived at the wall around the abbey churchyard, by which time it was truly dark and no moon had yet arisen to give any sign of encouragement. But the abbey churchyard represented yet another type of terror, for he always had feared to go in there at night since the older boys had told him of how the wicked would rise from their graves at midnight to bewail their fate. Exhaustion overcame him, and he could no more step through the churchyard to get to the houses on the other side as he could have trekked all around it. Fearing that the dead would soon be waking, he lay down on the grass beside the wall and hoped to sleep.

This time there was no dreaming of Betty, for every time the wind stirred the grass he feared it was a dead man's dry skin rustling in the wind. Then the old abbey clock tolled midnight, each solemn clang like a repeated invitation to further terror – calling the dead out of the damp ground. He forced himself to open his eyes, forced himself to look around and prove himself braver than the old stories – but oh! In the dark of the night he saw a thin, white shape, hardly the body of a man but something formless and shape-shifting, moving quietly up the path to the abbey door! The gosherd thought immediately of

'In the dark of the night he saw a thin white shape...'
(Illustration by Jo Galtrey)

stories of wicked monks, condemned to an eternity of repeating their old monkish processions just as this weird shape was doing now.

The ghostly apparition seemed to wend its way to the abbey door, then moved sideways and, to his terror, seemed to stoop down and sink into the ground behind a tombstone. Had the ghostly monk returned to his grave in the dank fenland soil? Then there was silence.

All seemed quiet and midnight had passed, so the gosherd finally dragged forth sufficient courage to stand up and steal across the churchyard. He would have to pass near the spot where the ghostly form had sunk into the ground, but the danger seemed to have passed…

He tiptoed along the path, almost past where the shape had disappeared. Suddenly there was a movement and a white form seemed at and around his feet, reaching out with white talons towards him! The boy thought again of the stories he had been told – of boggarts and ghouls that came out of the grave to drag the living down to Hell with them. He thought of all the bad things he had done, or had intended to do.

'Our Lady, defend me from harm!' he shrieked, and then he prayed to the town's saint, 'Oh Guthlac, keep me safe.'

Crowland's famous bridge

Yet his pleas were in vain, for the apparition suddenly reared up at him and uttered a piercing and demonic hiss. The gosherd swooned, collapsing to the ground in an insensible heap.

When he came round it was already after the first light of morning and the churchyard seemed serene and peaceful. Beside his head was a pile of newly dug earth, and the gosherd realised he had collapsed beside a freshly dug grave – ready for the funeral that day. He clambered to his feet and, as he did so, looked down into the muddy grave – wherein sat the cause of all his problems, the old gander. It looked sideways at him from a jaundiced eye, then turned away to peck for worms; 'what a fool,' it seemed to be saying.

Author's Notes:
This story is taken from one of Thomas Cooper's poems, The Gosherd's Song. It is recounted as a tale told at a Christmas feast as 'a tale of merry Lincolnshire.' Cooper probably wrote this in the 1830s, possibly while living at Lincoln. Cooper was a Gainsborough man who became famous as a Chartist journalist but he always retained a love for the stories of his native county.

Crowland Abbey was a lonely and frightening place, even in the gosherd's day, but after Henry VIII's dissolution much of it was abandoned and it became an even more sombre site.

Chapter Three

Tales of the Poachers

Poachers certainly belong to a book about tales of the dark, for not only did they do most of their work at night but they also committed some fairly brutal and unpleasant deeds. The Lincolnshire Poacher is more or less the 'official' poem and song of the County, albeit other counties have sometime adapted it for their own purposes. No-one knows how old it is, but it was being printed and sung in the 1770s and was said to have been a favourite of George IV. The most legendary Lincolnshire criminal was indeed the poacher, although one enduring aspect of this figure's appeal is the 'popular' view that somehow poaching did not constitute a crime in the same way as – say – robbing a shop. The landowners had a different opinion and the draconian Game Laws of the 1820s created a mood of underlying violence. As the poem shows, for the ordinary young man poaching was often as much about excitement and a little profit as it was about desperation and survival; but there was also an element of 'taking from the rich' in the style of Robin Hood – though not always to give to the poor.

A Lincolnshire man could hunt almost anything that crept, ran or flew, but the pheasant became the most popular target – they were easy to get, and they ate other men's grain. Perhaps the change in the law of 1765, which eased restrictions on hunting 'conies' (rabbits) was an attempt at diversion, but the Game Laws of the early nineteenth century were seen as vicious and turned popular feeling against the landowners. Henceforth anyone who got away with a bit of poaching gained an aura of heroism.

Thus emerged the tradition of the 'honourable' poacher, such as Latimer 'Blucher' Lee, who started poaching while still at school in the 1840s. He was still at it in 1901, aided by a skilled dog that roamed far and wide ahead of him on the look-out for keepers and policemen.

A poacher apprehended.

One day he was walking back into Grantham after a night of poaching and stopped to pick up a big bag of onions – only to be arrested just after for stealing the onions. This was an irony that he played up to in court, in front of the magistrate. 'Stealing onions?' he blustered, 'Why, I'd scorn to do such a thing. You all know what my business is. I'm a poacher. I won't lower myself to onions!' And the case was dismissed.

This view of the poacher as honourable was even lauded in The Times, which in 1891 praised the 'sturdiness and solidity of character so graphically expressed by the Lincolnshire poacher [which] is an ingrained trait of our English rural life.' In fact, the reality was a little different, and poaching took up an inordinate amount of the police force's time (at ratepayers' expense) when this had previously been done by gamekeepers. The police had a struggle to control the poachers, and we might take an example from Stallingborough in 1885.

PC Carter saw William Thompson and two other men out in a field with dogs at night, and gave chase; Thompson hit him over the head with a heavy stick, smashing his helmet and knocking him out. Since Carter knew the look and indeed sound of Thompson he soon got him into court despite alibis from his wife and other men, where the poacher's track record was discussed: two convictions for game trespass, one for night poaching, seven appearances before county petty sessions and four before Grimsby borough magistrates.

This time he was fined £20, or six months prison, but it is unlikely this stopped him! John Green of Broughton near Brigg, arrested for a similar offence, was even more violent; when surprised by Constable Sellars in a field, he managed to strike the policeman on the head with a heavy stick, wrestle his truncheon out of his hands, force him to the ground, beat his head with his own truncheon, stamp on his head and then, when the policeman tried to get up, felled him with a blow that 'rendered him senseless'. Such was the romance of poaching!

Poaching affrays sometimes ended in bloodshed and, sometimes, an execution

In 1877 a poaching 'affray' in the woods at Norton Disney ended with the death of a gamekeeper, shot at close quarters. William 'Slenderman' Clark was accused, although two other local poachers had strong reason for alleging it was the other who pulled the trigger. Although he denied it to the last, 'Slenderman' went to the gallows.

More typical was the battle at Boothby Graffoe in 1888 when a gang of four or five poachers out coursing hares were surprised by two keepers; there was a strong chance the keepers would recognise their 'habitual' foes, so a battle to escape took place involving sticks and stones, the keepers ending up battered and with broken toes.

A man-trap preserved by the Lincolnshire police in their museum.

At times poaching was conducted almost as an industry. In 1859 gangs of poachers were reported as 'denuding' the woods around Stamford and sending their illicit gains away in several cart loads per night!

In Sutton Bridge there was a famous poacher named Mackenzie Thorpe, who in his more settled years brought up a family in a council house. One Lincolnshire lady, Jean Taylor, recalls going to school with one of his daughters and remembers that he had a back garden full of wild sea birds. He used to make a living as a marsh guide and, according to rumour, do a bit of poaching on the side; at one time he apparently virtually lived on the marsh. Famous people who came fowling, like James Robertson Justice, used Thorpe as a guide and even Prince Philip came to visit him at his council home. The name of the street was changed to Royal Close after this.

Les Marrows, who lived in the north of the county, said that in his village there were many 'ordinary people' who, in the 1930s and 1940s, were often hungry. Many were therefore tempted to do a spot of poaching on the Carrs especially, but he could not recall anyone ever getting caught by the keepers, though there were occasions when poachers had to swim across the Ancholme to escape. However, Harry Bedford said that people he knew never shot as a commercial venture, but would take a brace at a time for their own pot.

Harry said that he was even taken out by his own Dad, though a rule was that you were 'on your own' if caught. Harry's poaching tips included: never shoot your way into a wood as you need to work back away from anyone who might have heard you; as you walked into the wood, you should mark the trees where the pheasants were roosting and then take them on the return journey. One of his techniques was to gas the pheasant with carbine. You put a lid on top of a long stick, some carbine in the lid and spat on it so that it gave off a gas. This was then lifted up and held beneath the sleeping pheasant's head, so that it fell off its perch. You could also use a bit of wire down a tube, tickle the pheasant's chest and then snap a noose around its head.

A gamekeeper and poacher pose for a photograph.

Another who learnt poaching 'at his father's knee' was Neville Marriott. His father was permitted to shoot rabbits, but somehow they always ended up with pheasant for Sunday lunch. At the age of eight his father took him out 'and from then on I carried a bag on my back two nights a week, sometimes with as many as six pheasants inside it.' When he was ten he progressed to 'trafficking' in pheasants, being required to cycle to Grantham with a dozen pheasants in a sack to deliver to a chip shop in Butcher's Row – yielding £3.10s. Some of this was spent on a pork pie from Watkin's shop, but the wartime queues meant that Neville was often shoved aside by burly women!

Tom Scarfe also confessed to doing some poaching around Welton-le-Marsh in the early 1940s, having been taught to shoot and ferret by his father. His girlfriend's father was a rabbit-catcher and pig-killer, who rather unexpectedly took him out for pheasants in the Park one night – Tom turned up in his best suit, and had to be found some wellies. This gang of poachers were not subtle; they simply shot the pheasants out of the trees; they made so much noise that the local constable complained it was 'like Dunkirk.' Tom found that you could sell a pheasant for 5s to an airman going home on leave – good income when farm wages were 28s a week.

Another self-confessed poacher from east Lincolnshire was Syd Robinson.

As he says, poaching was often motivated by need rather than greed:

'Farm workers years ago were a lot of people who did poaching. Out of work, no money, always looking for food, sometimes only one meal a day. Not like today when everyone gets dole money, I never did at the age of eighteen. That is the reason I started being a poacher. It was a very dangerous game, always a risk of getting shot.'

Syd would often go out on moonlit nights, creeping along the hedgerows with his mate and listening to the birds settling down at dusk. They were not the only hunters about, for 'Sometimes you would see Mr Fox stand on his hind legs to see if anyone was about but if I was down wind he would not know.'

One night they had a successful session with some rabbit nets and bagged a couple for the pot but they were spotted by some farmers and had to 'run for our lives'. They managed to get away by lying under a hedge at a crossroads, but the next day the police came to call anyway: they had been reported. Both swore blind that the poachers were not them.

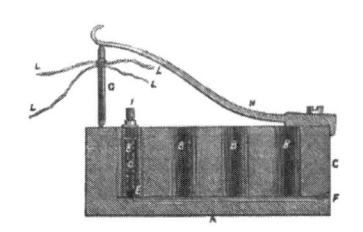

A Victorian alarm for scaring off poachers.

The police told them they were after two fellows who wore hob-nailed boots, so after they had gone the lads took their boots and buried them deep in a sugar beet field. Afterwards, they always wore wellingtons.

The two used to meet up out in the fields, using a code system. The first to arrive would put a stone on a certain gate post and hide a little further along until the other found the stone and joined him. One particular night they were after pheasants, but were unaware that the farmers were already hunting… them! However, the friends had a clear strategy worked out in advance; as soon as they were discovered they fled in opposite directions and then fired their guns as a signal that they had got away. However, this narrow escape convinced them that a poaching life was too risky and they vowed to 'go straight'.

A few days later both lads were asked by one of the farmers, in blissful ignorance, to help him take up his sugar beet crop. The farmer complimented them on being 'good hard-working lads', little knowing their nefarious activities.

There were many ways of poaching, usually with a good haul of pheasants being the aim. Two men could go into a field when the pheasants were roosting at night, and trail a net across the crop which was hiding them. It was a simple matter to startle the pheasants so that they flew up and got caught in the net. Another trick was to use old-fashioned dried plums or raisins threaded on a horse hair; the pheasant would eat along to the first fruit, but in trying to get the second would be choked by the hair.

Some poachers went after rabbits, of course. A trick here was to go out with an old battery, rather like a car battery, strapped to your back with a spotlight at the front; you could transfix a rabbit in the beam and a dog could be trained to sneak round to catch the rabbit.

At one village in the north of the County there was a notorious local poacher who eventually became a gamekeeper. Perhaps this was a good thing, as he also had a reputation for poaching other men's wives! As with many poachers, he went about by bike, had a 'day job' as a farm worker, and a colleague who teamed up with him for nocturnal ventures.

When this individual got a job as gamekeeper he knew all the local details and tricks, but quite a few people knew about him too!

Author's Notes:
The tale about 'Blucher' Lee comes from Shooting's Strangest Days by Tom Quinn. I have also used various contemporary press sources and some interviews with Lincolnshire folk, conducted about ten years ago. There are, of course, enough Lincolnshire poaching stories to fill a whole book.

Chapter Four

Satan's Cunning Plan

Hundreds of tears ago, going to church was an important weekly activity in every village in Lincolnshire, including Dorrington. Indeed back in the time of the first Queen Elizabeth it was a required activity – you could be fined if you did not attend, and churchwardens had real power. This was all very well if you happened to have convenient church in the middle of the village, but not so good if the church was a mile or so away.

Dorrington Church - but why is it so far from the village?

Now, at home in Dorrington Grandfather Cheffing had been put in charge of his grandson, Edmund, because the child's mother – his daughter – was away down the Sleaford road to Ruskington to help her sister who was due to give birth any day. What you needed when you had a child to come was someone you could trust, like your sister, and who did not cost money, so off she had gone although she no longer had a husband alive to look after her own child.

Grandfather knew it was a cold and wet Sunday the second he awoke, and the child had snivelled and fretted all night. The prospect of getting a bad-tempered six-year old up the road and up the hill to sit in a cold church was not a great one, but the old man had missed church the week before and knew the wardens would be keeping an eye out for him. The mention of going to church produced the expected reaction from the child: downright refusal. The old man thought carefully, and gave his response.

'Well, of course, Edmund, that is exactly what Satan is hoping for.' He made this observation while stirring the contents of his bowl, which were a bit colder than he would have liked.

The boy did not reply immediately, but Grandfather could tell his childish curiosity had been aroused. Eventually he spoke.

'Grandfather, what has it got to do with Satan? I just don't want to walk all that way to sit in a horrid damp church.'

'Exactly,' said Grandfather, 'and that is exactly what Satan is reckoning on you feeling. But you need to see that for centuries the people of Dorrington have been locked in battle with Satan, and he hasn't beaten us yet.'

This had the boy confused, because although he had heard strange tales of witches and even of dark creatures that could get you if you went out into the fen at night, he had never seen nor heard of Satan in a battle with the villagers. So he asked Grandfather what he meant.

"Grandfather, I don't want to go to church in this rain."

'Well,' said Grandfather, 'it is a bit of a long story, but it might be worth telling you.' Indeed it might, he thought to himself, for this way he might get the boy to church.

'The story starts a very long time ago, back in the days before even the Romans came this way. In those days the hill where the church stands did not have any church, but the old tribes used to meet there to worship whatever they worshipped and to sacrifice whatever they sacrificed. In fact I have heard tell that they used to sacrifice little boys who were badly behaved, so that the others would be good, but I don't know that for certain.'

Edmund curled his bottom lip at this. He loved his Grandfather, and the way the old man sometimes teased him. This time he wasn't quite sure whether this was tease or truth, but the old man went on with his story.

'Well time went by and the Christian missionaries came past these parts, bringing The Truth with them. But folks round here were a bit lazy and a bit short with their money so they never got round to building a proper stone church until those Saxons or Normans got here, at which point they began by thinking where to build one. I've been told that it was a lord named Tochti who had the idea, but not everyone agreed as some still worshipped in those old pagan ways. The village elders or whoever got together and discussed it, and all of them agreed they would build it down by where the houses are – and of course you know the houses are here because that's where the water is.'

The boy interrupted. 'But Grandfather, that's not right. The church isn't by the houses at all.'

'Exactly,' said Grandfather, 'and can you guess why that might be?'

Edmund put his thoughts together. 'Because of Satan?' he speculated.

'Correct again,' the old man said. 'Satan did not like the idea of the Dorrington folk having a nice, convenient church because his plan was for stopping people going to church. So, on the first day the men set to work building the church in the middle of the village; they dug the foundations and laid the first stones – which they had carted a long way at great effort – into the ground. By evening they were really pleased with themselves and they went off with the stonemasons to have a few beers and then for a good sleep.'

'The next day they were up with the sunrise to resume their work. Of course, it wasn't very far from their front door to the building site, and it took them only a few seconds to get there - but rather longer to recover from the shock of what they found. The stones they had laid so neatly had disappeared and the foundations they had dug had been filled in! There was no sign of their stone, or even their building tools!'

The boy reached his own conclusion. 'Was it those bad people from Ruskington? They've always been jealous of our having a better church than them.' The old man shook his head and the boy tried another idea. 'Could it have been...Satan?'

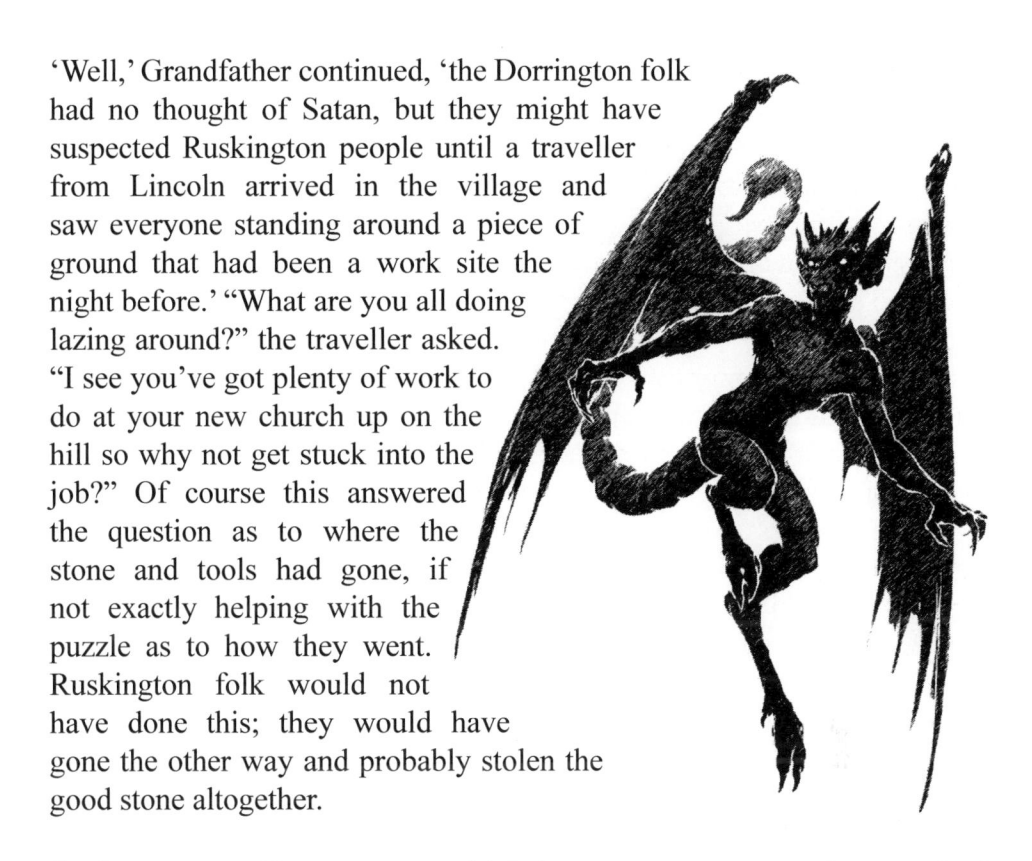

'Well,' Grandfather continued, 'the Dorrington folk had no thought of Satan, but they might have suspected Ruskington people until a traveller from Lincoln arrived in the village and saw everyone standing around a piece of ground that had been a work site the night before.' "What are you all doing lazing around?" the traveller asked. "I see you've got plenty of work to do at your new church up on the hill so why not get stuck into the job?" Of course this answered the question as to where the stone and tools had gone, if not exactly helping with the puzzle as to how they went. Ruskington folk would not have done this; they would have gone the other way and probably stolen the good stone altogether.

So there was nothing anyone could do but get a cart out, get the stone back, and start again on the site in the middle of the village. After which, they all went back to bed – quite exhausted.

Well, that night the same thing happened; all the work they had done during the day was undone, and instead apparently redone at a different site up on the hill a mile out of the village. So this time they knew exactly where to look for their stones and tools, and started to think that there was more to this than a prank by rival villagers. So the wiser ones amongst them began to think what they might do, and the first idea was to watch over the events at night to see what happened.

So that night a few of the braver souls hid in a ditch from where they could see the work they had done in the day. Just after midnight, when there was not a sound in the air and only a thin moon peeking through a bit of cloud, they heard a stirring in the old oak tree. One man nudged another and told him that he had always thought owls lived in there, but it wasn't an owl that came out.

The old man paused, enjoying the boy's suspense.

'No, not an owl, but Satan himself! And not only Satan, but a whole crew of imps dancing behind him!'

'Imps!' shrieked the boy, mixing terror and delight. 'Were they the same imps that caused such trouble in Lincoln?'

'Well, I reckon they probably were,' Grandfather mused, 'excepting one of course, who I think caused no more trouble after that day at the cathedral. Remember, this was before the saintly Hugh had the cathedral rebuilt. Anyway, Satan got them working away and in no time at all those imps had dug up all the stones and carried them away through the air to the hilltop. The braver ones amongst the men – perhaps that Tochti chap included – made their ways up the hilltop and hid in the hedge although I think that Satan knew they were there all the time anyway.'

' "Now then my imps," Satan said, "that's it for tonight's work then and we will see if that sorts them." One of the imps was a bit braver and thought to ask his master why exactly they were building a church, that not being their usual line of work. As you can imagine, Satan was not best pleased with this and called him all sorts of names your mother would not want to hear. Then Satan explained his plan, that the Dorrington folk were such a spineless lot with little faith in Christ and so a few hundred yards of walking was all that was needed to put them off going to church. The old man paused for his key point. 'A bit like you, really, Edmund.'

The boy furrowed his brow. He was starting to think he was a bit tougher than that.

'So', the old man continued, 'the villagers wondered what to do. They had a priest of sorts to turn to, but he was a bit limited in terms of real schooling and they didn't see him as much of a competitor with Satan, albeit he might have known a words of Latin. So they got themselves together and went off to see the monks at Bardney, they being reckoned to be the top people locally.'

'Well, when they got there they expected to see the Abbot personally but he was often away doing business, so they ended up with what they thought to be a simple old man. They could not see the old man as being likely to come and fight Satan for them. They got a bit bad-tempered, but in the end a bit of common sense prevailed, so they told the old monk their story. At the end of it he smiled and said nothing for a few minutes. Clearly he was thinking of an excuse to get away from them – they thought.'

'However, the old monk spoke up. "Who is greater – God or Satan?" the monk asked. They knew the correct answer to that one – God. The old monk nodded, and asked another: "Which is greater, your faith in God or your faith in Satan?" Now that was a bit harder, because one or two of them thought they had seen Satan the night before but they did not think they had ever seen God. Nonetheless, they knew the correct answer. "In God, of course," they told the monk. Well, the monk shook his head. "Satan seems to think differently," he said. "He thinks your faith in God is so feeble that a few hundred yards of walking will discourage you. Is this true?" Well, the men of Dorrington were outraged at the line this was taking, and most violently declared they had strong faith in God. "Well, then," the monk explained, "beat Satan at his own game. Let him build the church on the hilltop and then attend it every week, whether it is sunny, raining or snowing. That way you win, and you also save yourselves some work."'

'Well, they all went home chewing this over, and by the time they had got back to Dorrington most of them agreed the old monk's answer was very wise – all except one of them, who had married a young wife and did not want to get up early on a Sunday morning. So that is why the church is where it is. They left it there and Satan finished the job, and have been faithfully attending it ever since. In fact, it is a matter of great importance to Dorrington folk that they continue to go, for some have said that the Sunday no-one attends, Satan will come back again to take us for his own.'

By the time the old man had finished his story, Edmund had his coat on. 'Come on, Grandfather,' he shouted, 'we don't want to be late for church!'

Author's Notes:
Long, long ago, in the turbulent centuries between the Romans and the Normans or just after, the lands of Lindsey and Kesteven were often a battleground between all sorts of forces – some of them good, and some of them bad. In lots of the stories that have trickled down to us from those times, there is a struggle between Light and Dark, none more famous than the story

of the Lincoln Imp himself; the story of how Satan tried to stop the building of the Cathedral is so well known that I won't repeat it here, although you can read about it in Tales of Old Lincolnshire.

Less well known is that the Devil did his best to interfere with the building of any church, not just the Cathedral, and the story of the Church at Dorrington illustrates the point. We don't know when this story started to be told, and I have interpreted how it might have been told at one point in the past. I have also added a few details to explain why the Devil was apparently allowed to get his wish.

At one time I used to drive past Dorrington church on my way to work every day and enjoyed its lonely isolation on the small hilltop. In fact, a hilltop location is not unusual in Lincolnshire and nor is an isolated church, of which there are lots: Walesby and Sempringham are two of my favourites. Even in the village where I grew up, Dunholme, the church occupies the highest point in the surrounding landscape, albeit not exactly a very high point. Opposite Dorrington church used to be a wooden house, almost a chalet, where the famous pioneer of jet engines Frank Whittle once lodged. This sort of juxtaposition of old and new worlds is a very Lincolnshire characteristic.

Chapter Five

Death in the Wash

The coast is a major part of Lincolnshire life, so we need to have at least one story about it.

Although the North Sea and the Wash have provided much stimulus to the Lincolnshire economy both through tourism and fishing, they are fickle friends. Even for those such as seamen who were intimately acquainted with wind and tide, there were risks, such as in December 1827 when the barque *Ceres* was wrecked between Boston and Wainfleet Haven with the loss of five lives. Untrustworthy winds and tides also caused major boating disasters off Skegness and Mablethorpe. In 1885 the *Olive Branch* capsized off Mablethorpe and five drowned; local fishermen said the boat had not been properly 'trimmed', implying bad seamanship.

In Lincolnshire, many shipwrecks occurred within sight of land

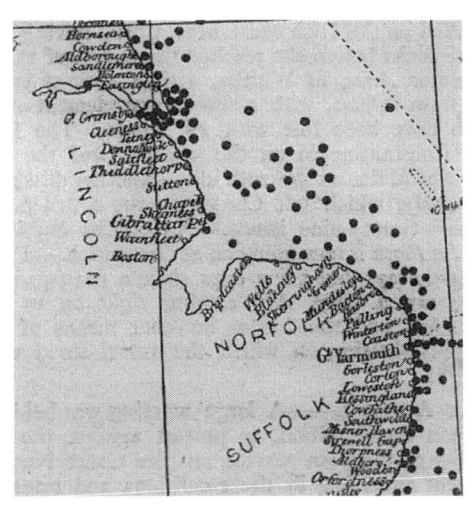

A map of wrecks in 1873 showing the perils of sailing in The Wash

Twenty-six drowned in 1893 after a squall capsized a boat full of London railway workers, which had gone out to Boston Deeps. Five drowned in 1895, when a pleasure cruiser from Hunstanton foundered in a squall off the Lincolnshire coast. Two yachtsmen died in June 1896; having left Boston, their yacht drifted onshore near Skegness with no sign of them. It was later discovered that they had gone ashore near Gibraltar Point in a canvas rowing boat and been lost on their way back to their yacht.

The North Sea and the Wash have proved treacherous friends when it comes to pleasure bathing, bringing tragedy and despair to many families. For as long as there has been sea bathing people have trusted to the waters of the Wash, and trust has sometimes been misplaced. Long before people went to Skegness, locals went to Freiston Shore, and a pleasure bather drowned there as early as 1808 when the idea of voluntarily putting yourself into the sea for pleasure was just getting started.

In the past, attitudes to health and safety were rather different. In the 1800s it was possible to take a steamer trip from Boston to the Bar Sands in Boston Deeps and, at low tide, get out and walk around. In 1887 one young man who did this wandered off from everyone else so he could go for a swim, leaving only his clothes behind; it was reported that his loss 'cast a gloom over the other excursionists'.

Pleasure seekers often went out in small adapted fishing boats

The Skegness coast is deceptive: with a smooth beach and gentle angle, it can appear safe, but powerful currents regularly overwhelmed incautious visitors.

Cartoonists had fun with the inexperienced on the beach

Accidents while bathing became quite common. In 1889 a young schoolmaster was seen in the sea at 7.30am when, despite being in only three feet of water, he appeared to stand up and call for help before disappearing back into the water – all in front of his fiancée watching from the sands.

When his body was examined there was no sign of drowning – it was found he had died of a heart attack.

In 1895 two young members of the Grimsby Primitive Methodists' choir were carried away by an undercurrent at Mablethorpe; one was rescued but the other drowned.

On many occasions it was not just the bather who drowned, but sometimes it was the rescuer. In 1930 railway clerk Percy Bailey was walking at Skegness when he saw two brothers, art students from Nottingham, getting into difficulties. Though a noted athlete but not much of a swimmer himself, Bailey plunged into the heavy seas and managed to drag one of the brothers to safety. He then returned for the other, but his efforts had tired him and he got into problems himself. Another man, Carter, who was sitting on the beach with his wife, then swam out to try to rescue Bailey and managed to get hold of him; however, Carter's collar became twisted and threatened to choke him, so he momentarily let go of Bailey – and in that moment lost him. Another man from London then joined in the rescue attempt and managed to get the semi-conscious Carter ashore. Bailey died, but both brothers survived. This was the second tragedy that week at Skegness.

The waters of the dykes and rivers leading into the Wash have also been a famous attraction for winter activities including skating, all of which were also attended with risk. In 1831 a child drowned at Frampton near Boston when he fell through the ice; he was able to cling onto the side while others ran for help but a local man refused to lend his boat and despite the efforts of the constable the child died. The coroner was unable to punish the heartless individual but thought that his feelings on what had happened would be 'sufficient punishment'. Another boy drowned at Boston in 1858.

At various times of the day or year, the saltmarshes and mudflats of the Wash can appear a benign place, especially when the sun is shining and the birds are singing. But those who know it well also know that it can be a place where it is easy to stray into danger. A friend of the author's tells a story of how, as a young man, he waded out too far to do some fishing and was caught by the tide coming round behind him, seemingly cutting off his route back to solid ground. Only through luckily stumbling into shallower water did he manage to drag himself back to safety.

Swimming in the rivers and dykes was – and is – dangerous. Typical was an accident at Corporation Point near Boston in 1877 where a young man 'suddenly dropped out of his depth'. This type of problem gave rise to one incident that was especially famous at the time though largely forgotten now. Kirton Skeldyke is a remote hamlet where a network of lanes eventually leads down to the old 'Sea Bank' and, beyond that, into the saltmarshes and creeks of the Wash or – more exactly – the mouth of the River Welland. Here, in 1902, occurred one of the saddest tragedies of this treacherous area.

Local families often went down to Kirton Skeldyke for an excursion. The Tomlinsons were a farming family who lived nearby at Kirton Holme, where Jabez and his wife Charlotte had brought up a family on the land. However, farm employment was not what it had been and the family had scattered around the country; but in August 1902 there was something of a reunion, perhaps partly because one of the cousins, Ada Mumford, had come visiting from London with the young man who was to be her husband.

So, on 25 August the Tomlinsons organised a party to go to the 'seaside' at Skeldyke. With them was Ida Clayton, aged twenty-two, the daughter of another local farmer, and housekeeper to the Tomlinsons; Mark Tomlinson, their son, twenty-four, who was an attendant at the City Asylum in Nottingham, Ada Mumford, twenty-five, who lived in Peckham; Edith Goodman, of Kirton Holme; and Arthur Strange, her fiancé, who was said to come from Paddington where he worked as a carman.

Down by the water's edge all relaxed, but soon the younger ones wanted to do something and so the young women put on some old clothes so they could play a game of 'following the tide'. The idea was to wade into the water as deep as you could go – up to your armpits – and then to slowly follow out the ebbing tide. Ida and Ada set the pace, soon being out in the water with it swirling around their chests and armpits.

Unfortunately, the mouth of the Welland was a very different place to a beach like Skegness. The water was muddy and its bed could not easily be seen, especially when in depths of around five feet or more. Suddenly the young women stepped forwards and their footing gave way beneath them; in an instant, both were off their feet and losing control in the surging water. Later reports suggested they had stepped into a 'quicksand', but it is more likely that they had stepped into the deep water channel.

The young women screamed and Arthur Strange, who was the closest, pushed his way forwards towards, them followed, rather less effectively, by old Mrs Tomlinson. Strange was seen to grab hold of one or even both of the young women, but the next moment he disappeared from view as he, too, lost his footing in the channel.

Mark Tomlinson also arrived to give help, but he, too, was swept away with one of the young women. Some reports said that the struggling of the girls was too much for the young men and they were dragged down with those whom they fought to save. Both the old parents and Edith Goodman waded in as far as they dared – up to their necks, some reports said – but could do nothing further to help.

The memorial, in London, to Tomlinson and Strange.

The body of one of the women was retrieved fairly soon afterwards, two others within a day or two, and finally Arthur Strange's body was recovered. Inquests were held by the Coroner, Dr Arthur Tuxford, and the jury requested that notices should be put up warning that bathing was dangerous.

There is a largely forgotten memorial to the tragic heroes of Kirton Sheldyke – more than a hundred miles away in the centre of London. The artist George Frederick Watts had got the idea for a Memorial to Heroic Self-Sacrifice in what was known as Postman's Park, close to the old General Post Office site in the City of London.

The memorial was opened in 1900 and one of the earliest was to Arthur Strange and Mark Tomlinson, who were recorded on a ceramic plaque to have given their lives 'in a desperate venture to save two girls from a quicksand in Lincolnshire' but 'were themselves engulfed'. However, they were slow to receive commemoration as their ceramic plaque was not unveiled until 1908, by which time Watts himself had been dead for four years and his wife had taken over the project.

Drownings such as this and the beach incidents have continued in the area. Only a few miles north at Wilson's Creek, Friskney Flats, two step-brothers of eighteen and twenty drowned after one got into difficulties and the other tried to help him in 1933; their uncle also nearly died in the rescue attempt. On a number of occasions, such as at Ingoldmells in 2001, it has been the man going to the rescue who has drowned, although in 1938 a man was able to rescue a drowning woman at Skegness by riding into the sea on horseback.

Chapter Six

Captain Spitfire

The Fifteenth Century was a challenging time to be alive and even more challenging if you wanted to advance yourself in wealth and social position. Disputes over the throne had led to endemic chaos and disorder, so it was said that dark characters such as pirates and brigands roved the Lincolnshire coast looking for whatever and whoever they could despoil. The government was too weak to stop them.

However, Sir William Hussey had done rather well for himself through a career in the Law mixed with a little politics. Although he kept an impressive fortified house near Boston – the Hussey Tower – he was increasingly in London as he advanced to be attorney general, and so kept a house there as well. His growing influence was cemented when his oldest daughter, Elizabeth, married the Earl of Kent, and he had high hopes for his second daughter, Mary.

But Sir William was often in London with his wife, who judged that the beautiful Mary was still too young at sixteen to be brought out into London society. So she was left in Boston, being considered quite old enough to run the Tower House there, although she had the help of the elderly and sober seneschal, Roger.

Hussey Tower stands on the edge of Boston, where in later years it became a sorry ruin

This was despite the well-known problems of the 'freebooters' – piratical smugglers or smuggling pirates – who roved the seaways of the Lincolnshire coast and sometimes ventured inland as the Vikings had done before them.

Now the government finally stirred itself and decided to appoint someone to protect the coast, and this commission was taken by a young man who became known locally as 'Captain Spitfire'. Spitfire was a young man who was as handsome as he was well-mannered, and at first he was widely celebrated in the town – he was even invited to Hussey Tower during one of Sir William's visits. Spitfire was reported to be a nobleman, though no-one knew this for certain, and to have powerful friends 'at Court'. During many a banquet he was able to thrill the local people with tales of maritime bravery, but tales of quite another sort also began to spread, and as a result his invitations to polite houses began to dry up. It was reported that Spitfire and his young crewmen were overly fond of roistering and that, as far as young ladies were concerned, he had wandering eyes and hands to match. So mothers of young daughters became more circumspect and, though they loved to talk about him, they did so only when their daughters were out of the way.

Spitfire was soon out and about chasing freebooters and pirates, but when he came to harbour in Boston he heard tell that the most beautiful girl in the town was Mary Hussey. So he took to calling at Hussey Tower, but every time he went he saw only the fierce Lady Hussey, who previously he had thought to be always in London.

Spitfire had a conference with his young second officer, Jack Bang, as a result of which the latter set out with a few gold coins and some honeyed words to charm Lady Mary's maid, Alice. With Alice hooked, Spitfire was able to find out whenever Mary was due to leave the Tower and so could manage to 'bump into her' along the way – the way which often took her to the Friary, as she was very religious having been largely brought up by the nuns of Stainfield. Now, it is sad to report that Spitfire's intentions regarding Mary were neither honest nor decent, but in these repeated brief meetings he came to respect her strength of character and virtuous approach to life.

As befitting a lady, Mary had her own confessor, the rather stout Sacristan of the Austin Friars, Father Adam. Had Lady Hussey or her daughter spent longer in Boston town, they might have heard more about Father Adam and have known that he was not a wise choice; one who knew this very thing was Alice the maid, having had some personal experience in the matter, but it was a topic in which she felt rather compromised and so she held her tongue.

For the truth was that Father Adam was a lascivious old rogue, the sort of irreligious character who inveigled his way into holy orders because he knew what to say and how to say it, but whose heart was elsewhere entirely. Father

Adam had a rather liberal interpretation of the vow of chastity (namely that it applied to other people), aided by some of the luxuries to which he had access, and then chance had delivered this rather credulous young woman into his confessional!

Adam plied Mary with sanctimonious words which were designed to make her reliant upon him. Yet one day the maid Alice herself went to see the old rogue, who was at first delighted to see one of his former 'interests'. 'Don't get any ideas,' she told him forcefully, 'and don't get any ideas about Lady Mary either. I know you, so listen. Mary has someone powerful watching over her and if you harm her, you will pay dearly for it.'

Friar Adam spluttered and protested but Alice was made of stern stuff. 'Do you think I have forgotten that nonsense you tried on in the elm grove by the fish pond? Or the disgrace that poor Bridget Welburn had to endure when she told everyone she had fallen pregnant by a monk? So don't try anything.'

Now Father Adam was rather confused by these words and thought that Alice had herself become very religious. Well, if God was 'watching over her' it mattered little as the burly friar already had a few offences stacked up against his name and one more would matter little.

While all this was going on, the Lady Elizabeth and her noble husband came to visit, bringing lots of young hangers-on with them, who enjoyed a good time rather too enthusiastically. This was too much for the seneschal, Old Roger, who favoured a sober and orderly way of life. He was shocked when the Earl recounted how they had visited the Pope, kissed his feet, left a gift, and been absolved of all past and future sins. This was not the sort of thing he wanted his beloved Lady Mary to hear, and he was glad when they left.

A few evenings later a veiled Lady Mary left the Tower and walked quietly to the Austin Friars' building. As she did so she had a sense of being watched or even followed, but every time she looked around she saw nothing but the bushes moving in the breeze. When she got to the Chapel, Father Adam offered her a drink – a cordial – which he said would ease her tensions and make her more open to spiritual insight. Mary drank down the cordial and Father Adam ushered her into the confessional, where she knelt down and promptly fell asleep.

The burly friar planted a kiss on the top of her head and then waddled off to get help. He returned with another man, the porter, and together they carried her outside towards the river. Near there was an old doorway leading down into 'St Austin's Grot' – what had been a cell used by a hermit, but was now more commonly used for punishment and isolation. Only the porter had the key to the rusty gate, and it was the intention of Father Adam that they should lock the girl down there for his nefarious purposes.

A lascivious monk is a stock character in British legends.

The two men laid the comatose girl down on the damp grass to force the gate open, but just as they did so there was a sudden movement from behind and within seconds they had been pushed forwards and tumbled down the steps into the darkness. Then the gate clanged shut behind.

By the next day there was some consternation at the Tower. First it was discovered that Lady Mary had vanished and, after a while, it was also discovered that her maid Alice was missing. After much searching, someone mentioned that Lady Mary liked to go to confession every day so a messenger was sent to the Austin Friars – and came back with the news that the confessor and the porter were missing as well! This triggered a search of the whole town, which eventually led to the discovery of shouts coming from the old grotto.

Out came Father Adam and the porter. The first was raving and delusional, but in a rambling way he mentioned Lady Mary. The porter told a tale about Lady Mary having fainted, and Father Adam having asked him to carry her to a safe place…before they were attacked and the lady taken. This tale sounded a little unlikely, so the porter was put under more pressure and eventually admitted that he knew about Father Adam's habits. The porter started sobbing for mercy, and said that he thought Satan had punished them and an angel had carried Mary away.

Lady Mary, though, awoke not in Heaven but in a small room lined with wood…that was moving. Her distress was increased by loud, thunderous noises above and the face of an ogre of some form, who appeared through a door. Then, slowly, her mind came to life and she recognised herself as in a ship's cabin. Next she heard the voice of Alice, speaking to the ogre, and was comforted.

Alice told her that she and Captain Spitfire had been worried about Father Adam and had vowed to protect her – sometimes innocence and trust were not enough in this wicked world. However, in her own way Alice had also been tricked, as Captain Spitfire and his accomplices had taken both women to their ship – not to the Tower as promised! They had been taken out to sea and in the Deeps had suddenly spotted the *Kelpie*, the vessel of a notorious Scottish pirate. For hours the battle raged, and it was not going too well for Captain Spitfire. The Scots were well-armed and fierce, and they had better guns, so Spitfire decided that a direct assault was the only plan left – he would move in close and board the pirate ship! They threw across the grappling irons and began to prepare for combat hand-to-hand.

After three boarding attempts were repulsed, the English crew finally managed to get onto the Scottish decks and the pirates scuttled below. Six of the cunning Scots then crawled out of the portholes of their ship and into the portholes of Spitfire's ship – and then the grappling irons broke. The ships drifted apart, with the Scots on the English ship and the English on the Scots ship.

The coast around Boston was wide open to depredation by Pirates.

Spitfire stood dumbfounded on the Scottish decks, realising the terror of the situation. Indeed, he then heard the sound of women screaming; for certain the pirates would have first gone to ransack the captain's cabin and discovered the women. Spitfire, Jack Bang and seven others reacted by doing the only thing they could; they dived into the sea and began swimming to their own ship before the distance became too great. As they did so, shots rang out and there were more screams.

"There stood two women, pistols in each hand..." (Illustration by Jo Galtrey)

Spitfire scrambled up onto his own ship, the rest of his men just behind, and was confronted with an astonishing sight. There stood two women, pistols in each hand, and with two bleeding corpses at their feet. In front of them cowered four pirates, like wolves at bay. Thinking the arrival of the English a distraction, one of the pirates chose this moment to grab at Lady Mary's outstretched hand – and without hesitating she shot him dead.

Since Lady Mary declined to stay at sea a moment longer than necessary, they were soon back in Boston and news was sent to her worried parents.

By this time it had become clear to Mary that Captain Spitfire was deeply in love with her, and that Alice and Jack Bang seemed well-acquainted. Mary's parents were delighted to have her back, gave their consent to a marriage, and within three days Lady Mary and the dashing Captain Spitfire were married without anyone really knowing much about who he was. Jack Bang and Alice were also married, though with rather less ceremony and rather more ale, and of course this meant that Alice had to leave Mary's service.

A few days later the happy couple set off for their new life together, Captain Spitfire telling his new wife that he had a little land to farm and look after between his naval exploits. On the way across southern Lincolnshire they came in sight of Grimsthorpe Castle. 'Let's call in and see if they will offer us refreshment,' said the gallant Captain, and so they rode up to the castle gates.

Lady Mary was rather surprised at how quickly the gates swung open, and how easy it was for them to ride in. She was even more surprised when they were greeted by Jack Bang and Alice, 'Welcome to your new home, my lady,' said the former naval assistant. 'I am the steward of this fine estate.'

And so the truth was revealed to Lady Mary, who found that she was now 'Lady Willoughby'. 'Captain Spitfire' was really the noble Lord William, but he had vowed to do something for his country and to set aside his titles so that he could win his true love through genuine feeling rather than pride and flattery. Perhaps, though, Sir William Hussey had known a little of 'Spitfire's' antecedents before agreeing to such a hasty wedding. Lady Mary moved into Grimsthorpe Castle and enjoyed a few years of happiness there with her dashing husband.

Hussey Tower in later years

Author's Notes:
This is the first of two stories adapted from Traditions of Lincolnshire, supposedly written by 'Roger Quaint' and published in 1841. Despite the title, the stories in this book are mainly about the Boston area. Quaint describes himself as formerly a monk of the Grey Friary, Boston; however, he uses this tale in the book to make a number of very derogatory comments about the Catholic faith, which I have mainly amended. This is a rip-roaring story, but rather cavalier with the facts: yet there is a kernel of truth in it that may have been subsequently mythologised in the telling! There certainly was a Sir William Hussey, of a Sleaford family, who was Attorney General in 1471-8; he did have a daughter Mary who married William Willoughby, who became 11th Baron Willougby d'Eresby in 1499, although it was Willoughby's second wife – Maria de Salinas – who proved more pivotal. Mary died without children. Grimsthorpe was granted to them on the second marriage in 1516, so Quaint's chronology is clearly wrong. Elizabeth also did marry the Earl of Kent.

However, 'Quaint' gives Captain Spitfire the surname of 'Bertie' but this name did not enter the history until later when Catherine Willoughby, the widow of the Duke of Suffolk as well as being Baroness Willoughby d'Eresby, married Richard Bertie; he was from Southampton and his father had commanded a fort, so perhaps this is where the idea of coastal defences came in! Hussey Tower was built about 1450 for Sir John Hussey.

From which we might conclude that this is a good story…but not very true!

Chapter Seven

The Maddening Member for Lincoln

Charles de Laet Waldo Sibthorp was the rather impressive full name of Colonel Sibthorp (1783-1855), a famous or perhaps infamous MP for Lincoln. He was well known at the time for extreme hatred of 'modern' life and perhaps had 'something of the night' about him. Although perhaps not really a creature of the 'darkest' hue, he certainly contributed to an image for Lincoln and Lincolnshire as being rather 'backward' as in the sense of 'benighted'. The Sibthorp family were not Lincoln people in their origins. They were descended from Hugo Sibthorp of Laneham, just across the Trent in Nottinghamshire, close to which was the small hamlet of Sibthorpe, but they later became synonymous with Canwick, on the edge of Lincoln, following a bit of judicious marrying into families with more land and money.

The infamous Colonel Sibthorpe

As a second son, Sibthorp chose to pursue the military option to provide for himself. After a largely domesticated military career, with some service overseas in the Peninsular War, Sibthorp took over the family estates in 1822 after the death of his brother Coningsby. In between he married the daughter of an Irish MP.

Sibthorp first became MP for Lincoln in 1826 and held the seat almost continuously, apart from a hiatus in 1833-4, until 1855, when he was unseated by death. He took over the seat which had previously been held by his brother, his father, his great-uncle, and his great-grandfather. However, his death proved to be only a temporary hesitation for the

43

Sibthorp dynasty, since his son Gervaise then took over the constituency.

Sibthorp's political career got off to a poor start when he was knocked down by an object thrown at him on his first appearance at the hustings. Despite this, he was duly elected. His views were decidedly conservative, although of a peculiar type. His political philosophy seems to have been that life had reached a point of perfection in about 1800 and nothing that came thereafter could possibly be any good. This included fashion, so he stuck steadfastly to the coats, boots and glasses of his favourite era.

He was said to resemble Charles I with 'a constitutional sadness of temperament' and a 'look of predestinated misfortune'. He was also a noted exponent of what would now be called 'bling', wearing very large gold rings and a hefty gold chain from which dangled gold seals and other items.

He hated the idea of political reform and strongly opposed the 1832 Reform Bill. This was not always as conservative as it seemed, though, as he worried the division into two of the Lincolnshire constituency (which was separate from Lincoln itself) would create a 'pocket borough' controlled by Lord Yarborough. However, he could show support to the disadvantaged, was instrumental in a move that helped the poor widows of clergymen, and spoke up about pensions for soldiers of lower ranks compared to wealthy officers. He disliked the idea that minor tradesmen in towns might be able to vote but not substantial tenant farmers, but typically made his point in insulting terms for those who dwelled in towns:

> 'When the new Bill was to have that influx of people from the small boroughs, those multifarious classes of voters out of the Cholera Morbus places—when they were to have such people, why was the right of voting to be refused to the healthy country farmers?'

Sibthorp's views on reform did not win him unanimous support, as might be imagined. A typical reaction occurred when he got up to speak and 'was for some time inaudible, in consequence of a general fit of coughing which seized the Members sitting on the Ministerial side of the House'. Sibthorp replied that 'He was an independent Member of Parliament, and would do his duty, let them cough as they liked.' He also contributed vigorously to a debate on corruption, wanting to know the boundary between hospitality and bribery. He would have been an ardent opponent of 'lobbying' today and questioned 'the dinners given to Ministerial Members in Downing-street, and the feeding and fattening of them by his Majesty's Government, that they might have their votes, [which] were indisputable specimens of corruption'.

A satirical cartoon portraying Sibthorpe attempting to control the trains

Also in 1832 he opposed the Anatomy Bill as he thought it unfair that those who died in hospital should be consigned to dissection – a 'brutal act.' He volunteered his own body for dissection – 'though it is not worth much' – and then showed his own peculiar brand of reaction:

'...in his opinion, crimes were not punished with sufficient severity—especially those most rascally of all criminals, horse-stealers, who were tried at every Assize, and yet rarely ever got hanged, which they richly deserved. The bodies of persons of that description should be dissected.'

At the same time, he opposed the emancipation of slaves in the colonies but also argued for tough penalties on the owners of ships that foundered through negligence, often causing the loss of scores of lives.

His conservatism did not make him a slavish devotee of the royal family. In fact he first achieved national prominence in 1840 when he argued against a vote of a £50,000 to Prince Albert on the grounds that it was far too much; he proposed a motion for £20,000 less. Due to the machinations of other political groups, Sibthorp suddenly found his motion had an expected popularity and it was pushed through to Queen Victoria's chagrin. It is often said this is the reason why she did not visit Lincoln whilst Sibthorp was its MP.

Sibthorp was not a total reactionary and, unlike many other members of the country gentry, was not bothered about defending the Game Laws. In April 1842 he took against the comments of the MP for Durham during a debate and lampooned his suspected hypocrisy. 'He wondered whether if the intelligent farmer in Lincolnshire offered the honourable member for Durham a cock pheasant, would he object to it lest it might have been poached [laughter]; or if he made the honourable member a present of a brace of hares, would he inquire whether they had been snared, or killed legitimately by the consent of the owner?' [renewed laughter].Sibthorp went on to say he 'cared nothing for game' but 'if he caught the honourable member for Durham amongst any of the preserves in the county with which he was connected, he should not be the last to assist in apprehending him and taking him before a magistrate, in order that he might be fined as such an intruder deserved.' [great laughter]. This sort of knockabout humour goes a long way to explaining Sibthorp's popularity. He also won popular sympathy by opposing the Poor Law arrangement by which elderly married couples in workhouses had been forced to live separately.

The Great Exhibition of 1851 and its associated Crystal Palace might almost have been invented to cause Sibthorp apoplexy. Apart from being promoted by the foreign Prince Albert, it opened on Sundays, celebrated modernity, and encouraged the lower classes to travel. Sibthorp condemned it as 'a great fraud upon the public' and said that its contents were mere 'trash and trumpery' – although he had not been to see.

Though Sibthorp prayed for fire to fall from heaven it did not, nor is there any evidence that the voters of Lincoln did not mingle in Kensington with the thousands of other visitors. Mind you, Sibthorp did not reserve his ire against shows just for the Exhibition: he also denounced the National Gallery as a waste of money, and suggested demolishing it; during the same year he also campaigned against large advertising vans and barrel organs.

Almost automatically Sibthorp was opposed to 'free trade' and favoured protective duties to keep out foreign goods. 'The Government has encouraged foreigners to that degree,' he said in 1853, 'for durability, solidity, and beauty, there was nothing like the British manufactures.' He was a real John Bull. He had no reliance upon the French. 'Beware of man-traps and spring-guns in Prussia and Austria.' Sibthorp here showed a real Lincolnshire interest in the tools of the gamekeeper! He also detested government officials of all sorts, and was unhappy about plans to set up a committee to consider official salaries: 'It was his painful duty to say that he looked with extreme suspicion upon all official men; and in such a case as this it was not likely that they would cry 'stinking fish.''

Sibthorp is still infamous today for his hostility to railways, for which he was heavily lampooned at the time. However, what he really hated was the idea that a private company could get legal permission to take a man's land off him and build a railway on it. Although the *Dictionary of National Biography* claims that he 'was instrumental in preventing Lincoln from being served by a main line', the remoteness of the city from major industrial areas was just as instrumental a fact, and nor was it entirely true: the 'loop line' of the Great Northern briefly put the city on the main East Coast route. It was ironic that his body was taken back to Lincoln by train on December 21, 1855. However, he also opposed a roads planner in 1830 as 'whom he took to be one of those visionary gentlemen who expected to feed upon the public'. One of his first utterances on this type of issue was actually to oppose the use of steam vehicles on the roads in 1832, which he thought would injure agricultural interests.

Sibthorp died in 1855, when he was summarised by *The Times* as 'the embodiment of honest but unreasoning Tory prejudice; down to the very last he showed himself a politician of the extinct school….' Nonetheless, he retained his popularity and the funeral at Canwick saw great crowds anxious to glimpse the coffin. He was promptly replaced by his son as MP for Lincoln

– Major Sibthorp. The son was elected without an election, he being the only proposed candidate, and with a nomination from Lincoln's mayor.

So why did Sibthorp manage to retain the affection – it would seem – of at least some of the Lincoln people? He did have an eye for a popular topic: for example, in 1830 he demanded harsher penalties for those who adulterated ordinary people's beer. He also was a witty speaker; indeed, the *Guardian* said that 'the Colonel never spoke [in Parliament] without raising a laugh, and frequently got up for no other purpose.' In fact he was so legendary that people started to laugh as soon as he rose to his feet, before a word had been spoken, but some thought him guilty of deliberately courting the press with speeches that would make good copy. The *Guardian* concluded that he was in fact 'a weak politician and a puerile speaker.' So despite his opposition to anything modern, Sibthorp managed to retain enough affection amongst his local people to stay in Parliament, but it did not do much for the reputation of Lincoln!

Author's Notes:
Sibthorp is believed by many to be the inspiration for the character Lebedev in the classic Dostoyevsky work The Idiot. There is nothing in this account, I hope, which is not true; yet Sibthorp attained a legendary, almost mythic character in his lifetime and after death. It was reported at his death that he was famous throughout Europe and when foreigners visited Westminster he was the one they asked to see, after the Prime Minister.

Chapter Eight

Love, Death and a Maiden

It was midnight, and the broad full moon poured out her silver imitation of noon across the Lincolnshire countryside. The white light above Gainsborough picked out, likely ghostly sheets, the towers and battlements of the old manorial house, and cast from them long shadows like clouds on a stormy day.

On the battlements, the warder slept whilst on duty, with his hand resting on his sword, the night being so still he could not conceive of any surprise visit – you could hear a horse for miles. There was not enough breeze to ruffle the Trent or stir the leaves on the trees behind the Old Hall. Even the owl was silent, although just then a nightingale began to warble, singing a sad omen at the hour when the lady was to meet her lover.

The crenellated walls were pierced with loopholes, once used to cast death down upon besieging foes, but now only the lady's hand fluttered there while she watched and sighed. Sometimes sharply attentive, at other times trembling with doubt, she listened for any sound that could be her knight coming fast down the silent river. And then she saw it – like a winged hawk skimming the surface of the river comes the boat carrying her brave lover. It reached the patch of sand and he stepped nobly ashore, while the lady waved again with her delicate white hand in the moonlight. Then, breathing a hasty prayer, she softly glided down the stairs and stood at the gate where her own faithful maid stood waiting her instructions.

Together the two women struggled with the massive bolts that held fast the door, fearing lest the slightest sound awake the slumbering warder, but in a moment they had the bolts drawn back and the warrior knight embraced his love in the moonlight.

'Oh Agnes,' the knight prayed tenderly, 'will you not flee away with me this night? Quell your maiden fears and step into this skiff of mine, which is as fast as any on the river. To do so would bring great joy to this lonely heart of mine.'

Agnes rebuked him gently. 'Oh Romara,' she whispered, 'do not seek to break the heart of my doting father. If I ran away I should prove unworthy of his high hopes and count only as a defiled creature in his eyes. When he looks at me now I see fierce pride in his eyes but this would rob him of his pride. If, Romara, you love me truly then you would know not to be untrue to the holiest of laws.'

The knight calls up to his lady-love (Illustration by Jo Galtrey)

Romara took off his plume-crowned helmet, bowed before her, and shook with grief, knowing the hatred that her father bore for him. His lips could not speak the words, but his tears and hers mingled with each other's sorrows. And thus they stood at the gate, holding each moment as if it were the last, until the maid cried out, 'Lady Agnes dear, you forget how swiftly the moontide flies. That surly warder will awake and the morning dawns! My heart is shaking with fear – we will be discovered!'

But Agnes could not so easily be scared away from her handsome Romara, and she clung to him for precious moments. The maid became more agitated, pleading to the knight that he imperilled fair Agnes's very life. 'If this should meet her father's sight, by heaven, she will die!'

At this, brave Romara tore himself out of Agnes's arms and returned to his skiff, ready for the short journey back upstream to his castle at Torksey. Agnes returned to her bed, her cheeks flushed with excitement, but with the colours of rose and lily in her face, her father could look only on her with tenderness.

Meanwhile Romara had returned to his skiff, waiting on what had been the placid waters of the Trent. Yet now it seemed the very ocean had reached upstream and stirred its waters as the hoarse aegir roared its length, lashing at the banks with wrathful force. The young fish were stirred and thrown by the water, exposing them to the hungry jaws of the pike and the eel, yet through it all appeared a porpoise, snorting as if with laughter and riding the wave in quest of salmon to snack upon.

A similar tempest raged in the heart of Romara, so he paid little heed to the savage furrowing of the waters. His hopes and fears were set only on the image of Agnes Plantagenet. Though it was gloomy still and the mists of dawn hid the towers of Gainsborough, he fancied he could see her still, kneeling in the old chapel before the Holy Cross and no doubt praying that the watching saints would save him from a watery grave.

Just then Romara heard a deathful scream that recalled the shriek of a maddened bittern in misery for her perished brood of young. But the cry came again, and the knight this time recognised it as human – indeed, the cry of mortal man facing Death. The desolate cry pierced even the billowing sound of the tidal surge, so Romara guided his boat towards the source of the cry by the river bank and there saw a single man, clinging in desperation to a willow branch. Only his aged, silvery beard appeared above the wave and it seemed that his strength was all but gone – just one hesitation by Romara might have cost his life.

So Romara leapt to rescue the old man from the yawning tidal surge and hauled him into the skiff. The old man could say not a word as Romara stripped him of his drenched vest and wrapped his own warm cloak around him. Then, as morning light began to streak the waters the sun arose in the east and coated with garments of gold the towers of Torksey castle, Romara's home. As he hastened to moor his boat, dewy fragrances blew across from the fields on either side. Two serving men spied his approach from the castle towers and hastened to help him moor the boat, but found themselves with an extra burden. Romara gave his orders, and they carried with silent steps the rescued man to a soft and silken couch.

The servants, and Romara, gazed upon the sleeping man in wonder. He seemed to rest with such peace and serenity, suggesting a blending of the earthly with a heavenly spirit; Romara thought that he had only ever seen such beauty in Agnes' face before, yet this one was so different. A doctor was summoned, and declared there was no injury – he would soon awake. Romara set at his bedside, watching the peaceful eyelids gradually open; when they did, the old man uttered a lowly prayer of grateful praise, celebrating his reprieve from certain death.

Romara was full of questions. Who is this man, with his great serenity, as if he had a vision of the Virgin or received some message from the angels who dwell before the very throne of God in heaven?

'I hope, when I die, to see the angels too,' said Romara. 'I pray to their image and kiss their feet in the missal that my mother gave me, two days before she died. Pray, kind man, tell me of your own visions and dreams. Of what do the angels speak to you?'

Then the old man stirred from his bed and met Romara's gaze. But, in moments, the old man's face changed from joy to deepest grief, from radiant hope to dark portent of future ills beyond control. 'Son of an honoured line,' he said, 'I grieve that I can speak no words except of woe and fear. The sun is setting for you and your kind; you will have no heir and not even the feeblest trace of your good name will survive. Your love is fatal, and fatal too the brave act by which you rescued me, for there is none who can save you.'

Soon after the old man left the towers of Torksey and was seen no more. Its lord was bereft, yet, such was his spirit that he vainly built a shrine of hope in his heart that love, with faith, might yet defeat the grim king Death.

Mere miles away the dreaded Lord Plantagenet was also awake and stirred himself to go down into his deepest dungeons, there to count his imprisoned victims. Alone, carrying only a blood-red, flaming torch, he descended into the gloom and moved around the vaults as the captives cursed his evil name.

There was one vault, the deepest and direst, most lost in the gloom, that the lord was last to visit. This was the living tomb in which he had imprisoned his own father. Now he flung in some bread and water, shouting that it was merely the interest on the gold he had borrowed, but that soon he would cease to visit altogether. Then he laughed wildly and scornfully, the sounds echoing off the walls, but when he looked into the gloom there was no-one there to hear the hate and scorn.

This was a mystery, yet the other captives began to tell how an angel had appeared in the dungeons and led the old man to heaven. They did not know, and nor did the lord, that this angel had in reality been his fair daughter Agnes.

A few days later the Lord Plantagenet rode out with his men in mailed armour and a band of pipes and drums just as the dawn was breaking. They rode the few miles to Torksey and there his herald cried out from outside its walls, 'We come not as foes but in true faith to promise that you shall soon enfold your lover's charms and that Agnes shall be your bride.'

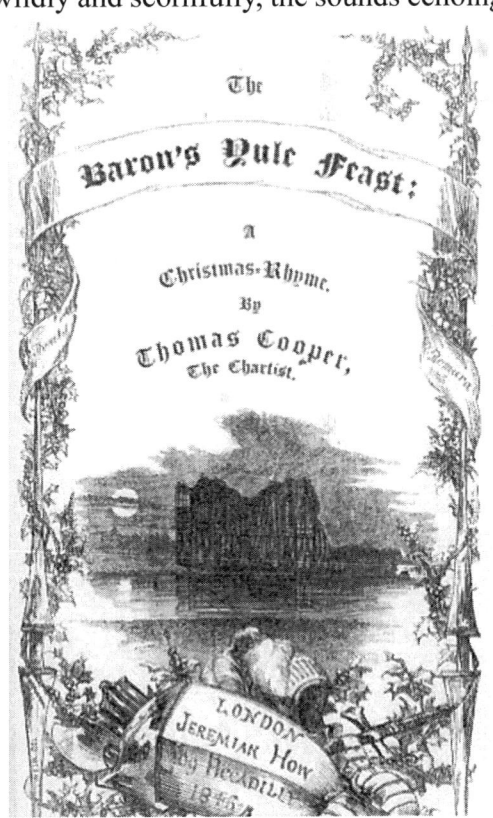

The title page of Thomas Cooper's Christmas book shows Torksey Castle

Just as he cried this news a raven croaked, but Romara was beguiled by the banners and music, and was deaf to the omen of the bird's call. His heart clinging to hope, he permitted the men to cross his castle's moat. 'Ride, ride,' said Plantagenet. 'The lady and the priest wait by the altar at this very moment.' Within what felt like mere moments they were at Gainsborough and the lord ushered Romara towards a downward stair. 'See here,' he said, 'in our family we say our prayers in the company of our ancestors in the crypt.'

And into dungeons they went, Plantagenet striding ahead, Romara behind, then the mailed men closed off any other route. In the red torchlight the faces of the sullen captives appeared, dazed and quaking at what might be happening, and then Romara saw the deathlike forms that they wore – strange wedding guests indeed. He recalled the old man's prophesy, and too late the truth broke upon him as he was pushed into a dank, dark cell with a chain hanging from the wall.

'Behold your bride,' declared the evil lord. 'Will you wear this wedding chain? This chain once bound my father here and he would have found his grave beneath the river's waves except your hateful hand intervened. So this chain shall now be your bride and this dank dungeon your marriage bed. And when your youthful blood freezes in death, my cry is that the fiends will seize your spirit.'

Plantagenet turned and left, but his minions knew his orders and they abandoned Romara in the dark cell with no food or water. His heart pined in dread and, within a few days, he was dead. Tearful Agnes was left to weep over his fate, but her father was so embittered that he could not even leave her with this.

'Take her to the old tower,' he cried one day, and the silent retainers held her firmly in their iron grasp as they went up the narrow stairs. Agnes knew the small room in the tower, but was shocked to find the windows freshly bricked up. As the key turned in the heavy lock behind her, she was wrapped in almost total darkness, never to be seen again.

Author's Notes:
The story of the Fair Maid of Lancaster, supposedly walled up in Gainsborough Old Hall by John of Gaunt has long been told in the town. I have used a version

as told by Thomas Cooper in a book of his poems from 1845 which ends with her lover dying in the dungeons though it leaves room perhaps for her to be walled up afterwards; it is certainly a dark and gloomy tale with no trace of a happy ending! Cooper was a famous Chartist writer who grew up in Gainsborough but later turned his talents to preaching. As far as possible, I have used the language and names he used though he freely admitted that 'Romara' was a name he had plucked from elsewhere in Lincolnshire. In his notes, Cooper explains that in childhood he was often told about how the fair maid was 'starved to death in one of the rooms of the old tower' because of 'her perverse attachment to her father's foe'. It is still a very popular tale in the town.

But let's have Cooper tell us himself:

"The very interesting relic of the Old Hall at Gainsborough is associated, in the mind of one who spent more than half his existence in the old town, with much that is chivalrous. Mowbrays, Percys, De Burghs, and other high names of the feudal era are in the list of its possessors, as lords of the manor. None, however, of its former tenants calls up such stirring associations as 'Old John of Gaunt, time-honoured Lancaster', who, with his earldom of Lincoln, held this castle and enlarged and beautified it. Tradition confidently affirms that his daughter was starved to death by him, in one of the rooms of the old tower, in consequence of her perverse attachment to her father's foe, the knight of Torksey. Often have I heard the recital, from some aged gossip, by the fireside on a winter's night; and the rehearsal was invariably delivered with so much of solemn and serious averment; that the lady was still seen; that she would point out treasure, to anyone who had the courage to speak to her; and that some families had been enriched by her ghostly means, though they had kept the secret, as to awaken within me no little dread of leaving the fireside for bed in the dark!

With indescribable feeling I wandered along the carven galleries and ruined rooms, or crept up the antique massive staircases, of this crumbling mansion of departed state, in my boyhood, deriving from these stolen visits to its interior, mingled with my admiring gaze at its battlemented turret, and rich octagonal window (which tradition said had lighted the chapel erected by John of Gaunt) a passion for chivalry and romance, that not even my Chartism can quench. Once, and once only, I remember creeping, under the guidance of an elder boy, up to the 'dark room' in the turret; but the fear that we should really see the ghostly lady caused us to run down the staircase, with beating hearts, as soon as we had reached the door and had had one momentary peep!"

Chapter Nine

The Man who fought the Darkness

It was the most audacious crime in the history of Lincoln, striking both at all that was held sacred and the thriving pilgrimage trade that sustained many of the city's people. The remains of the blessed Saint Hugh had been enshrined in the cathedral for near on 150 years, his body in a stone tomb and his head kept separately in a jewelled casket. The latter was one of the greatest treasures of the city, and twice a year it was paraded through the streets to celebrate the life of its greatest bishop, even though he was a Frenchman by birth.

Then one night in 1364, it vanished. Thieves had watched as the precious reliquary had been returned to the cathedral, and they had perhaps hidden inside to await their chance.

Saint Hugh peers down from the south-west pinnacle of Lincoln Cathedral

Then, in the darkness, they took the precious casket, and escaped across the fields to avoid being seen on the highways. What happened next has never been quite certain, but somehow the thieves left the head in the field and it remained to offer a clue to the pursuers as to where to follow. But so precious was Hugh's head, and so well respected by man and beast (except the robbers), that when it was found it was being guarded by ravens. Although Hugh was known to have been very merciful in his lifetime, his devotees were not so kind – and when they tracked down the thieves, they hung them all.

So why was this head and its precious casket so special to Lincoln? Over the course of history, the area that we now know as Lincolnshire has suffered many dark times, the invasions of the Vikings and the retribution after the rebellion against Henry VIII being just two examples. But the area has also been blessed by men and women who were prepared to stand up and fight against darkness and corruption, and there is none more famous for this than a Frenchman, whose death was commemorated by kings meeting in Lincoln.

Hugh was born in south-east France and, in keeping with his parents' habits, decided from an early age that he was going to be for God and against the Devil. Although stories that he was ordained by the age of ten are pushing things a little, he was a monk by fifteen and a parish priest by twenty. During this period he was pursued by an amorous woman, and took refuge in the Grande Chartreuse monastery.

Hugh came to England to run a monastery in Somerset called Witham, (not connected with the place or river in Lincolnshire, therefore). He had been recommended to Henry II, and the two men were to share much time and debate in succeeding years. At Witham he showed an early commitment to helping the poor and unfortunate, and to standing up to the greedy and rapacious. Possessing considerable personal charm, he was able to challenge King Henry who was diverting Church money into his own coffers. Nonetheless, the king favoured Hugh and wanted him to be a bishop, but it took the Prior of Grande Chartreuse's best efforts to persuade him. Even then, Hugh insisted on a free election by the Lincoln canons: he did not like the king having too much influence.

When he became Bishop of Lincoln in 1186, Hugh showed equal zeal for opposing corruption within the church. The Archdeacon of Canterbury performed the ceremony and demanded the customary gift of a horse; Hugh

Saint Hugh is a common sight in stained glass windows with his friend, the swan

offered no more for the ceremony than he had paid for his mitre, which was of the simplest kind.

Hugh planned to visit all the properties connected with his new role, including the bishop's manor at Stow. Hugh would have known that Stow was seen as the 'mother church' for Lindsey and even wider areas, and it was where St Etheldreda was said to have stopped overnight and planted her ash wood staff into the ground, from which sprung a miraculous tree; perhaps Hugh believed this to be the literal truth, or he might have seen in it a story of the planting of the Church into a new area. However, he was warned that the Manor's moat had been invaded by a huge and vicious swan which had driven away all the other birds, and that no-one dared act against it. The servants caught the beast and brought it to him but, instead of ordering it to be roasted he fed it on bread and it became his devoted friend – even cuddling up to him. The swan stayed at Stow when Hugh was away, but seemed to know when he was coming back by its excited flapping. When he slept there it would guard him zealously and was known to nip the legs of chaplains who annoyed him. After he died it remained on the moat, sad and lonely.

The Bishop's Palace at Buckden

Hugh was involved in several miraculous events during his life. In 1199 he was passing through the town of Cheshunt when people brought to his attention the case of Roger Colhoppe, a sailor who had become mad and violent. The bishop dismounted his horse, blessed some water with his sacramental ring, and gave it to Roger to drink. Hugh then read the first verses of the Gospel of St John and the sailor went peacefully to sleep; when he awoke, his mind was clear and he was cured.

Mind you, Hugh's behaviour was not always so moral. When he visited the tomb of St Mary Magdalene in France he appeared to be praying close to her remains – until the monks who were guarding it realised he had bitten off two pieces of her arm to take home with him!

Passing through Alconbury, Hugh was told about a dying one year-old child who had swallowed a piece of decorative ironwork. Hugh placed his fingers on the child's throat and gave his blessing and on the following Sabbath the child coughed up the piece of metal which was kept as a relic of the saintly churchman.

His journeys were not always entirely safe: whilst passing through the Holland part of his diocese he was attacked by a 'ruffian' with a sword, but saved by his cousin William, who pulled the sword from the man's hands.

On another occasion, in 1194, Hugh was at Buckden, where he had a house, and was celebrating Mass. A clerk in the congregation saw a male child 'of supernatural brilliance and whiteness beyond man's imagination' as Hugh elevated the Host. Now, this clerk was not there by chance, since he had arrived from Oxford having heard a heavenly voice tell him to go to Hugh and instruct him to – in turn – 'admonish earnestly' the Archbishop to reform the abuses that were going on in the Church. There was plenty of favouritism in appointments and a good few priests guilty of some carnal sins, but the clerk had hesitated to make the journey – until successive voices came to him urging on the task.

Hugh was not afraid of trouble, whether with an archbishop or a king. He often admonished Henry II and also Richard I, and he was shocked to discover that Henry's mistress 'Fair' Rosamond had been buried close to the altar at Godstow – so he had her moved. Hugh had a famously fractious relationship with the royal foresters as the forest laws were a source of much anguish for the poor. Hugh, calling them 'keepers', famously barred them from the King's room by saying, 'Keepers, keep out' and when the king himself muttered at this Hugh replied, 'This saying concerns you too, for when the poor whom these men oppress are let into paradise, you will stand outside with the keepers.' Hugh even excommunicated foresters who mistreated his clergy, including the chief forester: this caused a dispute with the king, but Hugh was able to use his wit and humour to defuse the crisis.

Hugh was also a famous defender of the Jews, who were widely persecuted. In 1189 he intervened in a situation in Stamford where Jews were being persecuted, probably following the death of a man, and this was at some risk to himself. There was a similar anti-Jewish riot in Lincoln, where Hugh again intervened.

The statue of Saint Hugh and his swan at Buckden

Hugh personally worked hard on building the cathedral from 1192 which continued until at least 1200. He made extensive alterations, repairing the earthquake damages and extending it eastwards. The choir, transepts and part of the nave all featured his own manual efforts. A hod which he had carried was said to have cured a cripple.

The cathedral was seen as a beacon of God's light in a dark world, and Hugh wanted to keep it that way. It was said that he worked and prayed to invite the Holy Spirit into the building, while the Dean laboured to keep the Devil out. Of course, it is still windy around the cathedral to this day, and those in the know understand this is the Devil – still stirring things up and trying to get in.

One of the finishing touches on the northern pinnacle of the west front was a statue of a swinesherd playing his pipes. The huge building project was always short of money as the people of the diocese laboured to match the project's needs, and Hugh was grateful for all he could receive. A young swinesherd of Stow kept a few of his coins to give to the bishop and Hugh, mindful of Biblical principles about widows and mites, ordered the statue to be put up to show his gratitude.

When he lay dying on his bed in London, it is said that Hugh uttered a chastening prophecy on the sons of Queen Eleanor, whom he labelled an adulteress. He condemned her for having left her lawful French husband to take on an unlawful English one, Henry II, and that all four of their sons would be wiped out at the hands of King Philip of France 'as an ox plucks out grass by the roots'. Indeed, already three had died.

The dying Bishop confessed that 'my evil acts are completely evil, but my good actions are not entirely so.' Dressed in a hair shirt, he knelt and waited for his death, praying to the last that 'it is joy to possess [God]; whoever receives him and trusts in him is strong

The Swineherd of Slow on the north west pinnacle of Lincoln Cathedral

61

and secure.' As he lay dying, King John visited him; it was even reported that the wily reprobate was distressed, but Hugh saw little reason to waste his dying words on such a man. Hugh then gave instructions about his burial, including that he should be buried in the simple vestments he wore at his consecration. After he died his corpse was disembowelled on the instruction of the doctors, since it would take several days to carry to Lincoln.

Saint Hugh holding his Cathedral - a window in the church in Austerfield

The body was then carried from town to town, the first leg being from London to Hertford, accompanied always with candles. It was said that the continuing flame of the candles was itself miraculous. Great crowds gathered at Biggleswade and many who were there heard a sudden crack as the crush caused a break in the arm of a poor man, Bernard. No doctors were available, so the man was taken home in agony, but during the night Hugh appeared to him and the arm was healed. Two nights later a tailor of Stamford, who had led a holy and devoted life, asked for permission to touch the coffin; he was allowed, and then prayed that God would take his soul to heaven – that night he died. Also on the journey to Lincoln, a knight's cancerous arm was cured.

The last overnight stop was at Ancaster, but when they reached the foot of Steep Hill the next day there was the most amazing assemblage the city ever saw. The kings of England and Scotland both asked to carry the coffin, though the latter was overcome with grief. Three archbishops and sundry other bishops and nobles were also in attendance. The city's Jews came out to mark the passing of their great protector.

When he was laid out in the cathedral, some noticed the unusual whiteness of his skin with just a touch of red, as though he were asleep and not just a corpse. A cry went up that a blind woman had recovered her sight, and clergy were sent to verify the facts. The huge crowd attracted criminals as well as the faithful, and one of these took the chance to steal a woman's purse; he was found a few minutes later, wandering around unable to see, holding up the purse and sobbing that he had stolen it and been struck blind by Hugh. The purse was returned to its owner and that instant sight was returned to the blind thief.

There then followed a series of miracles. A blind man, Simon, who used to stumble around knocking against logs and stones, was cured at the tomb one Whitsun, and was afterwards kept in the Dean's house for two years; an oddity of this case was that after his cure the man did not recognise the sound of voices previously known to him. A crippled woman named Mary was brought to the tomb in a basket, where she fell asleep and spent the whole night. In the morning she woke in agony: she could hear her bones cracking and feel her muscles being stretched as her bent and twisted legs came back to life. A young man afflicted with paralysis, who had lived in a hut in St Mary's churchyard in front of the precentor's door, was cured at Hugh's tomb – perhaps to the relief of the precentor! A mad girl of Wigford was cured. Many other cures of madness, deafness, dumbness and even cancer were reported, including a cure for one of the Knights Templar.

The campaign to have Hugh declared a saint started from almost before he died, but the next local saint was actually St Gilbert of Sempringham, who was canonised in 1202. Then England became too deeply enmired in the complex affairs of King John, but those in Lincoln kept a record of the miraculous cures that seemed to result from visits to Hugh's tomb. Gerald of Wales and Adam of Eynsham wrote biographies of Hugh and the latter gave a personal testimony to a commission set up by the Pope in 1219. They logged a number of miracles during Hugh's life and 29 that had occurred at his tomb.

Hugh was declared a saint in 1220 with his feast on 17 November; he had died in the evening of 16 November so for Church purposes this counted as the next day.

In 1280 a new shrine was built for Hugh's remains. King Edward I and Queen Eleanor were in attendance as the remnants were placed into a shrine so decorative as hardly to have met Hugh's tastes in life. The head came away from the torso and was placed in a separate casket, being credited with 'sweating wonder-working oils'. At some point a tooth became separate from the head. As we have heard, the head was later stolen, but almost all the assemblage was lost during the Reformation.

The shrine of Saint Hugh - as it was

Author's Notes:
There are some well-known near-contemporary lives of Hugh and also some more modern ones including D H Farmer's Saint Hugh of Lincoln. Others, short and long, have been written over the years such as C L Marson's Hugh, Bishop of Lincoln, although this shows little interest in miracles. Unlike some of the other characters in this book, Hugh was a real living person who had significant influence on the city of Lincoln and the whole country, but he seems to have been a little eclipsed in popular interest for a time by 'little' Saint Hugh who may not have existed at all, or not in the way related at the time. 'Big' Hugh really ought to be more important in the city's consciousness but we don't seem quite sure what to do with our British 'saints'. Here I have concentrated on the stories and miracles, some of which have greater basis of evidence than others, and I leave the reader to choose between them.

Chapter Ten

The Invasion of Barton

Nearly three hundred years ago the average person in Lincolnshire had a very tenuous relationship with what we might call 'current events'. Indeed, for the most part, by the time that someone in Gosberton, or Goxhill, or Goltho got to hear of any event of note it was unlikely still to be 'current'. People lived in 'blissful innocence' or 'benighted ignorance', depending on your point of view. Of course, back in the mid-1700s it was also the case that few could read, so they were even more dependent on what others told them.

One town that might have claimed to be a little better informed was Barton upon Humber. For one thing, it was close to the mail road that took 'the news' from London to Hull, and for another it had a bit of a coastal trade and those that travelled up and down the coast might bring snatches of information with them. And indeed they did, but any news that had a week or two's incubation in the mind of a hard-drinking seaman was likely to be well-fermented by the time it reached the ears of a Barton denizen.

Now, one day in 1745 'the news' reached Barton that the Scottish had invaded! This information probably arrived from a well-sozzled sailor in the coastal trade, perhaps accompanied by some coal from Newcastle. In the sharing over a pint or four in a Barton inn, the news began to reach epic proportions.

'Have you heard,' the publican soon passed on, 'that that Prince Charlie has invaded with hordes of wild Scotchmen? They are racing through the country, pillaging and raping, and then they are going to string up King George at the Tower of London!'

'Yes, but where are they and when are they coming here?' asked a frightened soul, and soon it was being said that the wild Scottish horde was already at York and heading south by the minute, combining lightning speed with the most efficient pillaging and ravishing.

One of those who heard about the marauding Scots was Timothy Kean, the town's diminutive barber, whose scissors were as sharp as his wits were blunt.

Timothy was soon telling all his customers about the danger facing Barton and, being rather timorous, was shaking and trembling while he was a-telling. As a result, a good few customers who he shaved and trimmed left with little nips and jags from which blood trickled, whilst those who came in for a 'bleeding' left rather more pale than usual.

Scottish soldiers saluting their Prince

'I have heard from a reliable source,' said the barber, 'that these Scots rob and ransack everything they can see. From the border down to York there is not a house left standing, nor a horse, cow, chicken or sheep to be seen. I have even heard it said that they have killed and eaten every single rabbit in Yorkshire. Every field has been dug and its contents carted back to Scotland.'

'Terrible!' exclaimed the old farmer who was having his hair cut, though whether this was a comment on the Scottish or the haircut was not clear. 'Well, I have sold this year's lambs and I can drive the sheep up into some quiet corner, so I shan't worry too much.'

This was not the reaction that Timothy was expecting. 'Not worry?' he said. 'You really ought to. Up Durham way I heard that the Scots even dug up the grass out of the fields and carted that off as well. Apparently they use it to make porridge or something.'

News travelled fast, and over in the tailor's shop of Jacob Grit, it was being churned over at great speed. Grit was a tall, thin and ascetic man who liked to look on the dark side of life and, in adopting pessimism as a way of life, was never knowingly disappointed. Unlike Kean, Grit had the benefit of a steady stream of female customers.

'Ah, ladies,' he moaned, 'hide away anything you have of even the slightest value. I hear these Scots take everything from the glass out of the windows to the shelves out of your pantry. Pots, kettles, clothing, necklaces – they will take it all. The town will be denuded!'

Well, the ladies shook their heads and checked their pockets, but Grit had only just got started. 'Now I don't know how to put this,' said the tailor, secretly exulting in a really worrying message, 'but I hear tell these Scots are no respecters of a lady's honour, if you understand me.'

'Not of our honour?' said the ladies, shivers running down their spines as they began to conceive the fact that the Scottish ransacking might not stop just at their houses but might involve rather more.

'Indeed not,' bewailed the tailor, 'they will come first for your drink, then your food, then your jewels – and then yourselves, your daughters and probably even your servant girls!'

By lunchtime the ladies of the town, and a few of the men, had got up a deputation to do something about it. However, apart from an old soldier with a wooden leg, and a retired customs official with a drink problem, they had not been able to muster much by way of a defence force. Eventually they had a bright idea to go and see one of the magistrates, and there demanded he send immediately to Lincoln for 20,000 men to defend the town from being ransacked and ravished by the marauding Scots. The magistrate had difficulty finding anyone to take the risk of going to Lincoln as no-one knew whether the Scots were already there, or indeed already anywhere else! As for the Constable, he was strangely nowhere to be seen.

Now, amidst all the panic there was a solitary voice that took an opposing view. 'Why would the Scots come here?' asked the town's miller, a rather jovial figure who nonetheless had a thorough commitment to the principle of profit – and panic such as this was bad for trade! 'Barton is hardly on the road from Scotland to London, so unless King George has decided to hide out in Grimsby, then I can't see they'd come this way – unless they were lost, of course.'

To the people of Barton this was treacherous stuff. Was the miller trying to lull them into false security so that his Scottish friends could more easily catch them with their treasures unhidden and their wives still asleep in their beds? 'Liar!' someone shouted, and then another called out, 'Hasn't he always been against the King?' And a third person, recalling a hard bargain driven by the miller the previous week, said 'Let's put him in the stocks – he can wait for his Scottish friends there!'

The road into Barton

Well, the miller could see how things were going, so made himself scarce on the excuse of checking his own wife was safe. People drifted back to their houses, began hiding their most treasured possessions, and went to bed not expecting to sleep. The two members of the 'defence force' camped out on the road from the west, which they reckoned the most likely to be used by the Scots; or rather, they camped out behind a hedge near to the road.

The next day dawned – and no Scots were in sight. Nor the day after that, and so the atmosphere of terror began to slowly abate despite the efforts of Grit and Kean to stir it up. But the tension was still below the surface, and a couple of the most refined ladies and their daughters found reasons to go to Hull or Louth to 'visit ill relatives'.

The defence force had taken to sleeping at night and so it was one morning that, when the shutters in the houses overlooking the market place were pulled open, there was a terrifying sight – Scotsmen had taken over the market place! They were figures of great fearfulness, albeit there only appeared to be three who were prepared to show themselves. But what a sight they were: bushy unkempt beards of fiery red, clothes that were ragged and seemingly stained with the blood of the innocent, and shrunken faces from which stared out wild and unblinking eyes as black as the sins they had doubtless witnessed!

In an instant, the town took these three to be just the vanguard of a much larger force which was doubtless camping outside the town in order to build up its energies for a dose of ravaging, looting, and worse. Doors were bolted, shutters banged closed again and the women all rushed upstairs to their windows from which they shrieked cries such as 'Murder!' and more. This led others to assume that there already had been several murders, and would certainly be others. In these houses men flung themselves into their coal cellars and barricaded the doors, leaving their wives to face the Scots with a broom in their hands, while those caught outside fled home as quickly as they could, though furtively taking to the back streets. These folk quickly became harbingers of doom, taking the panic with them to homes in High Street, Fleetgate and Newport.

There was no apparent sighting of any English soldiers to chase the Scots away, the magistrate had left town and the 'defence force' was probably still asleep. Someone started shouting, 'Send for the Constable!' After all, even though he could not shoot the Scots he could at least arrest them.

Now the Constable was several years past his best. Never a tall man, he had become decidedly short, with legs that clearly were not designed for speed. Running was out of the question, since he was also short of breath and given to panting desperately whenever movement was required. He was transfixed with terror when people began calling for him and, from the safety of his house, shouted out that he had no warrant by which to arrest anyone and would someone go to the magistrate if they felt it necessary. Then he went back to bed, making sure his bedroom door was tightly fastened.

Meanwhile, the three Scots were still in the market place, since their weary limbs had an aversion to any further movement. However, even they could hardly miss the air of panic and alarm spreading around the town, and so they decided that it might be wise to move. As they entered Fleetgate they noticed the *Ferry Boat Inn,* and noticed too that its door was open. In a moment all the fears of Barton's population seemed to turn to reality as the Scots started a campaign of plunder….

Two of them went into the old inn whilst the third stood guard at its door. The smell of food took them into the kitchen, where they began the pillaging by seizing some bacon and a few bottles of beer that their seasoned military eyes had scouted out. Their appearance was something of a shock to the landlord, a man who was well-used to his own liquors, and whatever he might have wanted in terms of payment was forgotten when the two Scots waved their broadswords and muttered dark Pictish oaths.

The landlord might have been transfixed with fear, but his wife was made of sterner stuff. She made a rapid exit from the back door, seeking help, and ran to her neighbour – none other than the miller, who had had such a narrow escape from the stocks. The miller grabbed a bag of his best flour, directed two assistants to come with him, and marched straight back to the *Ferry Boat.*

The sentinel at the front door was little use – he was almost asleep – and so the miller walked right up to the surprised Highlander. The miller swung his bag at the man's face, and it burst, showering him with flour; he instinctively put up his hands to wipe his eyes, and in a trice his arms were grabbed and pinioned. This caused a commotion, so the other two came rushing out of the inn and were promptly assailed by flour bags swung by the miller's trusty assistants.

Within a minute the miller had captured the entire invading army. Looking very sorry for themselves, but with a fresh dusting of flour, they were marched to the chantry, where they were locked up.

The news of the 'victory' spread like wildfire. Those who were previously cowering in their cellars suddenly appeared on the streets, looking very fierce and brave. Women stopped howling and prodded their husbands out to find out the latest news. The chief dignitaries of the town decided to hold a 'council of war' at the *George.* Groups of men formed themselves into armed bands equipped with ancient pistols, fowling guns, old swords, pitchforks, rolling pins and clothes props. They fanned out along the main roads into the town, telling themselves tales of what they would do to any more cowering Scotsmen. Indeed, as the day drew on and the Scots proved more and more cowardly by not appearing, the Barton mensfolk grew in bravery so it was a wonder to behold them.

The council of war had to decide what to do. And they didn't want to have to do anything. So they agreed that the three Scots were 'state prisoners' and sent

English soldiers escorting Scottish prisoners

a messenger by boat to Hull, where there was a garrison with a captain who might take responsibility. The barber and the tailor put the word about that the three men would be hung or gibbeted, if not hung, drawn and quartered, if not all of these and more. This prediction was confirmed by the arrival that night of the officer and some men, armed with muskets and looking very determined. In order to check the veracity of the reports, they went straight to the *Ferry Boat* and were seen no more than night.

The next day they marched to the chantry, unlocked the door and looked in on…an empty room. Above there was a neat hole in the roof, through which the cunning Scots had no doubt escaped. The soldiers made a feeble attempt at hunting around, then went back to Hull.

Years afterwards, whispers began to spread about as to how the Scots had escaped. Rumour had it that the miller's wife had been much troubled that three men might die as a result of her husband's intervention, and the night when the soldiers were drinking the town dry she had not been able to sleep. She reminded the miller that there had been no ravishing committed by the Scots after all, and there might not be any more ravishing of any sort in their house either if he did not ease her conscience by helping the poor souls. This may or may not have been true, but the miller was certainly heard to say on the odd occasion that he was glad there had been no hangings as it would have been a lot to pay for a visit to the *Ferry Boat*.

So the invasion of Barton came to an end and the town returned to its benighted slumbers until, sixty years later, it was no doubt transfixed with the terror of a possible French invasion…

Author's Notes:
This is a well-loved tale and I have started with the version from The Social History and Antiquities of Barton-upon-Humber which was published in 1856 and written by H W Ball and W S Hesleden. Stories of 'ignorant' locals are of course multiple, and this one reminds me a little of the famous story of Hartlepool where a monkey was assumed to be a Frenchman and strung up on the gallows – or so it is said. Ball and Hesleden refer to the story as a 'tradition' which 'appeared in print some time ago', so we may assume they did not believe it entirely, and yet they felt it important enough to form a footnote running across two pages of their book.

Chapter Eleven

Love, the Devil and Redemption in Old Boston

Long ago, in fact so long ago that the Normans hadn't yet arrived in Lincoln the Fens really were fenland and only a few who knew them well could live there or travel across them. Tough and ill-educated men eked out a life living in mud huts on whatever piece of ground was solid enough and far enough above the winter water levels to offer some degree of freedom from the endless damp. Civilisation had largely passed them by, for their company largely came from dogs, ducks, fish and the odd cow, not from human contact. Even the Christian missionaries had made few inroads: the approach by land was perilous, and the approach by water through the Wash more perilous still!

The land around the mouth of the Witham was nominally ruled by the Saxon King Ethelmund of Mercia, who had a 'palace' of sorts at Kirton, which was the only place that passed for a 'town' at that time. But most local people were old Britons, who gave the Saxon king little more than nominal attention, whilst some resented his rule most bitterly. North and south of there, men clung to a painstaking existence, living in mud huts on small pieces of higher ground which the Norsemen called a 'holme.' Near a crossing point over the Witham was one such holme called 'Icanhoe' – the ford of the oxen.

One of the two 'houses' at Icanhoe belonged to Harold Hopper, a widower and miller who lived there with his son Edwin and daughter Dora. He had a rather inefficient water mill, with a wheel that clacked around in a desultory fashion, depending on the whims of the Witham and its tides. Close by lived Leolf, a young Saxon cowherd who had sole responsibility for the king's cattle which lived in the fenland pastures around there. Being both a royal servant and a Saxon, Leolf felt himself rather superior to Harold and was always thinking of how to drive the miller away, although he maintained a parallel interest in the miller's beautiful daughter.

Leolf especially detested the water wheel, which sometimes clacked around all night and kept him awake. He did all he could on his visits to Kirton to stir up official trouble for the miller, even insinuating that he was in league with the local rebel leader, Alan of the Tofts, but no superior official took his hints. In truth Harold was useful to the Mercians, because he always paid his dues on time and was the only miller in the district, who else would want to live there?

One night Leolf was returning with his bullocks, as he was getting them ready to drive to Kirton. He was tired, and not cautious enough. One of the bullocks, infuriated by being pushed around, decided to resolve the problem by pushing him back and charged the unwary herdsman – who was pitched headfirst into the muddy and murky waters of the Witham. Leolf could not swim, and cried out for help as he floated out into the stream, sometimes swirling down again into its turgid depths. As he drifted past the mill, Edwin the miller's son happened to be working on the banks, and heard the pitiful cries. For a second he hesitated, then Christian love overcame tribal enmity and he dived into the waters, hauling the spluttering herdsman rather unceremoniously to the river bank and dumping him in the mud.

Then Edwin realised Leolf was in rather a bad way and, using his broad miller's shoulders, carried the man like a sack of flour back to his hovel. But it was a November night and no fire was lit; a man who had been in the river would surely catch a chill and die. So Edwin lifted him up again and carried him back to the family hut where at least there was a fire.

Leolf was feverish, and his life hung in the balance for more than a week. During this time Dora nursed him carefully, but said few words to him. Leolf, though, fell more in love each day. The girl seemed bashful, would never answer a question, and at times disappeared for hours without a word being said as to where she had gone. As he began to recover, Leolf suddenly went into a panic - the cattle! If they had strayed and died, he would certainly be executed; but the kindly Edwin had looked after them for him, knowing the situation, and had even arranged for the bullocks to go to Kirton market.

Now that summer Ethelmund chose to visit Kirton and stayed there several months, bringing his court with him. Whilst there he organised a campaign to drive away rebel Britons, but as soon as his soldiers gave chase they melted away into the fens. Amongst the retinue was his priest and confessor, the saintly Botolph, who was known for his long and bushy beard as well as his pious and modest habits. Botolph was tiring of the ritual and self-importance of court life. It had had its value when he was establishing the Faith amongst the Mercians but now things were settled he yearned for a more devotional lifestyle. What he needed was a place where he could set up a monastery, but it had to be a site that would not involve evicting anyone who lived there. As he looked around the fenland sites he chanced upon Icanhoe, where there was enough room for his plans without clearing away the two little homes. So he asked Ethelmund for a grant of the land, and this was ceded to him.

Within no time at all Botolph set to work and Harold, Edwin and Dora watched as masons and carpenters conjured up some marvels. Soon a little town started to grow around the monastery and Botolph set aside some land to serve the spiritual needs of the settlers with a chapel of their own. Strange to say, the traffic that supported the needs of Botolph's work was never once attacked by the rebels.

As the work was nearing completion, Botolph got into the habit of an evening stroll down beside the river from where he could see all that had been done during the day. It was a good chance to be quiet and commune with God, but one evening Botolph caught himself looking at the monastery and the little town and feeling pride in what he had achieved.

'No, Satan,' he cried, 'I will not be tempted by vain and boastful thoughts. I renounce your efforts!'

In a flash of red smoke, a horrible black figure suddenly appeared in front of Botolph. 'Renounce me, do you?' the figure smirked. 'Yet you can never defeat me!' And with that Satan leapt upon poor Botolph with the certain intention of dragging his soul off to Hell before he had the chance to confess his sign of pride.

Well, Botolph called upon the Lord, and so with supernatural strength of his own he wrestled with Satan along the banks of the Witham. Though Botolph was weak and Satan strong, God was stronger still and Botolph gradually began to win the contest. Satan started to puff and pant as the effort began to tell on him until, with a great shriek of exasperation, he disappeared in another burst of smoke.

"In a flash, a horrible black figure suddenly appeared..."
(Illustration by Jo Galtrey)

No-one in the little town saw the epic battle, but a few evenings later Dora commented to her brother about how windy it was around the tower of the new church. 'Yes,' said Edwin, 'I have noticed that too. It is almost as if Satan himself is trying to blow down the tower of Botolph's church.' And some say that he is still trying to…

Now, as we have heard, the British rebels had a young and dangerous leader, Alan of the Tofts, who was skilled in the arts of raiding and plundering. One night the rebels came raiding right up to Kirton itself – and chaos ensued! When it had all died down quite a few things were missing and one of them was the king's baby son, Ethelbert. Ethelmund was distraught, and went to visit Botolph to ask for his help in getting his son back. Botolph spent the next night on his knees, praying for the baby's return.

The next day a note was found pinned to the church door. It announced that the baby had been found – alive – and that it would be returned if safe passage could be assured. Botolph was the man who could assure this, for no Briton trusted the Mercian king. So Botolph arranged this with Ethelmund, who promised never to harm the man who returned his son, and a few days later a young man walked up to the gates at Kirton, and stood in front of the gatekeeper with a small parcel wrapped in sackcloth. 'I will give this to the king and no other,' said the man, but the parcel squirmed and cried, for it concealed the lost princeling. The stranger was ushered to the king, who almost cried as he was handed back his son, and then the guards moved to seize the man. 'No,' shouted the king, 'I gave my word to God, and Botolph. Let him go free.' And so he did.

Well, rumour spread that it was Alan of the Tofts himself who had brought the child back, but the gatekeeper denied it. 'No,' he said, 'this was no brawny warrior but a young lad no more than twenty-one, slim and wiry, but not one to wield an axe.'

By this time Dora had grown into a very attractive young woman, and Leolf and many another sought her attention and her hand in marriage. But Dora turned them all aside, showing little interest. Leolf discussed this with some friends from the growing little town and all agreed they were only being rejected because she must already have a lover – but who?

Leolf devised a plan: to watch over her day and night until he discovered the identity of the mystery suitor – for surely there must be one! So by day and night he watched the front of the house, but never once did he see an unexpected visitor. Then, one day, while minding his cattle, he had a bright idea – perhaps the visitor came by boat to the back! So that he night he watched and, indeed, a mystery man in a black cloak arrived by boat and walked with the girl along the bank. The way they walked so close told Leolf that this was no ordinary friend, but a lover.

So he got all the other hopefuls together, and the next night they ambushed the man in the cloak just as he stepped onto dry land. Dora screamed, and

Boston 'Stump'

the sudden flash of her eyes told Leolf that his own hopes were as dead as last year's lambs. The gang of young men marched their captive into the town and pulled the cloak off his face; he was young and handsome for certain, but who was he?

Leolf never knew who first said it, but suddenly the word went up, 'It's Alan of the Tofts.' Leolf looked him in the face. 'Are you Alan of the Tofts?' The young man nodded. So here was a prize indeed for which Ethelmund would pay handsomely, and within minutes a messenger was on his way to Kirton. Soon a messenger came back. 'Prepare a gibbet, the King will be here in the morning.'

By the next morning Ethelmund was in a rare state of excitement. For so long this Alan of the Tofts had eluded him, and he wondered what sort of a warrior he would turn out to be: burly, weathered, hulking shoulders of muscle perhaps with the dank smell of a fenlander. When Ethelmund arrived in Botolph's town he found all ready, a gibbet prepared and a captive kneeling in front of it. He cried with delight, and the captive looked up – with a face that caused Ethelmund almost to leap with shock.

'This is not Alan of the Tofts!' he roared with anger. 'You have been tricked! This is the kind soul who brought me back my son!'

Things were looking bad for Leolf and his friends, except the silent stranger chose now to speak. 'You are mistaken,' he said, 'for although I am indeed he who returned your child I am also Alan of the Tofts, standing before you. I restored your child because I war not with infants but with men.'

Now Ethelmund was a man of his word, whether or not he kept to it because he was afraid of Botolph, and he reached down with his hand to the kneeling captive. 'You have treated my son fairly, and so I shall treat you. Let us stop this talk of war, and find instead a way to peace.'

So Ethelmund sat down together with Alan of the Tofts, and they worked out a way to share the land in peace. The king granted Alan the freedom of the fens and the soccage of Fishtoft, making Alan effectively a lord of the manor under the king. Alan accepted this, and was free to marry his true love, Dora. As to Leolf, it is said that he threw himself back into the river and this time no-one came to rescue him.

Author's Notes:
I have adapted this story from Traditions of Lincolnshire, which was published in 1841 by 'Roger Quaint', who referred to himself as a monk of Boston. Quaint has drawn on oral tradition and made some assumptions, one being that 'Icanhoe' – the town founded by Botolph (or 'Botwulf') – was Boston, though it is now identified as Iken in Suffolk, although 'Boston' is indeed seen as derived from 'Botwulf's Town.'

The ODNB suggests there may have been two saints of this name, and relics of at least one of them were close to Boston at Thorney. It's also possible that Boston was named after quite another Botwulf, and perhaps not a saintly one at all! But it makes a good story.

Chapter Twelve

The Dark Arts of the Decoy Men

The 'decoy' was once a familiar feature of the English landscape and they were especially common in our region, being found across Lincolnshire, Nottinghamshire and parts of Yorkshire. But nowadays the word is known only in its use for 'to deceive' with little knowledge of what or who was deceived; the answer – ducks, perhaps millions of them! Nonetheless, the word pops up all over the place – there is an Ashby Decoy Golf Club[2] (which sounds a bit unsporting!) near Scunthorpe and just across the border a Decoy Junction in Doncaster.

One of Lincolnshire's greatest resources in the older days was its reserves of wildfowl attracted to the fens, marshes, carrs and coastline. Because this offered such a rich source of food and work, Lincolnshire men resorted to some dirty tricks when the Dutch engineers came to drain the wetlands and turn them into farmland.

For the men of the Fen and the coastal Marsh, wildfowl were a source of free food from time immemorial and men soon developed effective ways of 'harvesting' them. Over the years many ruses had been developed for catching ducks and geese, some sensible, and some outlandish. *The History and Topography of the Isle of Axholme* by W B Stonehouse describes how men had used baited hooks and an unpleasant trick of wading in the water with your head covered by a perforated wooden 'vessel' so the ducks could not see or smell you. There was also the 'stalking horse', which involved getting a horse to walk as near to the prey as possible, with its head to the ground to hide the movement of the gunman behind; this trick was still being used in the early 1800s. In another version, fenmen used 'shouts' or 'shallops' which allowed you to hide in the water, with all the appearance of a floating log and so get a good shot at the fowl. But most of the tricks had their limitations, most importantly that in killing one duck you scared the others away.

---

[2] At least the golf club has a sense of history as its badge includes a duck.

Down on the fens around Spalding and Crowland men worked in large groups on a 'drive'. These took place in the summer when young birds could not yet fly and the adults were moulting and not easily able to. Two long lines of net were staked out along a watercourse, narrowing into a triangular shape; then men in boats would beat the reeds and drive out the birds into the nets. It was said that one drive there produced 3000 ducks and at Deeping Fen a drive with 400 boats yielded 4000 fowl. This type of net arrangement may have been the type of decoy referred to at Crowland in 1432, when an armed mob attacked the Abbot's decoy and took away 600 fowl. In fact these drives were so successful that they had the effect on the fowl that trawling had on North Sea cod later: they began to run out until a law was passed in 1534 to stop the practice over the summer months. But in this system of duck harvesting lay an idea that developed, with a bit of outside influence, into the decoy.

Often it has been claimed that the first 'decoy' in England was probably set up on behalf of Charles II in St James's Park, London, in 1665. However, it is likely that the idea of the decoy was brought to England by the same Dutch engineers who drained the fens and marshes; it is believed that a decoy in Northamptonshire dates from the 1640s or earlier. Within a few years the idea had spread and there were at one time at least 110 in East Anglia, including Lincolnshire.

A decoy may sound like some rustic memory of simple country folk, but they were actually complex and sophisticated systems for manufacturing profit on an industrial scale; nor could you build them just anywhere. You needed 'a large pond surrounded by a wood, and beyond that marshy and uncultivated country.' It was important not to be near habitation as the birds liked to be undisturbed so they could sleep, but at dusk they would rise up to action for feeding, a time which became known as 'the rising of the decoy.'

Having started with these natural advantages, a decoy needed a fair amount of human design to make it work. Off the main pond would lead narrow canals or 'pipes', and as they narrowed they would gain a covering of netting suspended above on hoops. The channel narrowed to reach a net across it, blocking any forward movement. This end was called the 'purse'. The pipes could be up to seventy yards long and twenty feet wide, narrowing down to two feet; similarly they might have nets at eighteen feet high at the entrance, but two feet high at the end.

But, you couldn't have just one pipe: you needed a variety to take account of the changing direction of the wind. As an old sporting journal advised, 'the decoy man keeps on the leeward side of the ducks, to prevent his effluvia reaching their sagacious nostrils'. The men would need to be close by, so screens of reeds lined the narrow channels behind which they could hide, peering through holes the size of a shilling coin.

Ducks float towards a decoy

The birds were fed with 'hempfeed' to tempt them to enter into the canals and pipes. Sometimes feed was left out a day or two before the real operation began, to lure them back in bigger numbers. To aid the process, the men had their own specially trained fowl, the traitors of the duck world, who would lead their sleepy fellows into the narrowing channel in search of this food. These were indeed the 'decoy ducks' and up to fifty of them might be needed. If movement was too slow, the decoy men would slip a dog — 'a small water spaniel' — out from behind the screens or show it at the small gaps, and this would cause the birds to move forwards into the narrowing 'pipe'. The dog would lure the wild birds to their doom, but not the tame traitors. Once behind the birds, the decoy man could use himself by popping his head through a gap in the screen called a 'head shew' and block off the exit. The wild fowl would get caught in the net as they attempted to fly from danger, for it was well known that ducks always flow in the opposite direction from a threat.

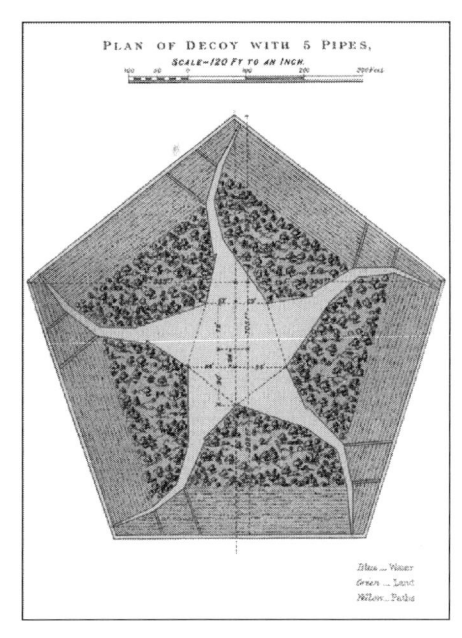

A decoy diagram

The traitors, though, were taught to dive down beneath the net and so swim their way to freedom. This explains why the decoy pipe was never straight: the ducks should not be able to see they were heading into a trap.

One bit of this needs explaining: the fact that the birds followed the dog rather than being chased by it. This is correct; the dog went along the bank and the wild ducks followed close by. There are all sorts of explanations as to why ducks would follow rather than avoid a natural predator, one of them being that the ducks fancied strength in numbers and also being able to keep an eye on what the dog was doing. It was, however, important that the dog was moving away from the ducks and if he turned and looked at them they would get nervous.

Skilled men learnt all the tricks of this trade: carry an ember of burning peat so ducks would not detect your smell; never speak when ducks were around; never catch the 'lead' ducks, or they would never return to the pond; communicate with your dog through signs, gestures and routines.

Typically, men could rent a decoy and try to make a profit by sending the fowl to London. At one point in the later 1700s ten decoys around Wainfleet were said to have produced 31,200 ducks for the London market but also a number of lesser-rated birds such as teal and wigeon, which were sold in Boston for ten pence a pair. Partridges were often caught in the decoy at Ashby. Geese could also be caught, being prized for their feathers, of which they were meant to be plucked alive.

A decoy man and his dog

During this time you could even be in a dynasty of decoy men. It was said that the Skeltons of Friskney spread across the USA in the early 1800s, taking their skills with them. Successive generations of Skeltons worked a decoy at Friskney, which was producing an income of about £700 a year from three to four dozen birds a day in season. At its peak it had six different nets but the Skeltons moved away, as agriculture encroached and the number of nets was reduced one by one. It stopped being used in 1878, but at one time there had been five different decoys around Friskney.

The 1830s seems to have been the last great decade of the decoys. At that time there were forty in Lincolnshire, including the famed two acre site at Ashby, which was said to have yielded a record 6000 fowl in 1834-5. In 1855 it was still being run by Henry Healey, who aptly resided at Decoy Cottage. Around Lincoln there were decoys at Skellingthorpe, which ran from about 1693 to 1840, Burton and South Carlton; experts claimed to be able to recognise where a duck came from in the county by its taste. In the north of the county there were decoys at Keadby, Ashby, Twigmoor and North Kelsey, but there were even more in the south where Dowsby caught 13,180 in 1765-6 and sold them at a dozen for seven shillings. There were three near Sempringham and the same number around Wrangle. The '600 decoy' at South Kyme was so-named as it was near '600 Farm' and Nocton Hall had a two acre decoy with five pipes in an ash wood.

The decoys went into terminal decline around the start of the nineteenth century. This was partly because of the encroaching of farmland, partly because prices were not high enough to cover the costs. In 1839 there was still one in 'occasional' use on Crowle Moor and another near New Zealand Farm. Stonehouse's elegant tones amply explain how the decoy was killed off: 'A small decoy yet lingers on part of the common, which remains uncovered with warp, where a few wild fowl are occasionally taken, just sufficient to remind the modern sportsman what a diversion the ancient fowler found in these extensive and wild resorts of the feathered race; and which now, by the ingenuity and labour of man, have been converted into a fertile and valuable soil, producing most abundant crops of grain, potatoes, and other vegetables'.

Author's Notes:
This is a perfect topic for 'darkest' Lincolnshire as the decoy was once so important, and is now so forgotten. Most people I speak to have little idea that they even existed. I have used several sources for this short look at a fascinating and forgotten topic. Stonehouse's History and Topography of the Isle of Axholme was published in 1839, but the Lincolnshire decoys were famous long before that as they were described glowingly in the Sporting Magazine of 1795. Sir Ralph Payne-Gallwey wrote his Book of Duck Decoys in 1886, by which time most of the Lincolnshire ones were a fading memory.

Chapter Thirteen

Escape from Lincoln Gaol

There are plenty of 'dark tales' about Lincoln Gaol, especially the 'old' one in the Castle where many executions took place. You can still visit the burial ground within the keep and see the stones, including that of Priscilla Biggadyke who was executed by mistake. But actually the most famous incident to do with prisoners in Lincoln was nothing to do with an execution, and whether you think it involves any 'dark' characters probably depends on your views about Irish independence. But it is certainly a story that involves deeds done in the dark!

The Irish republicans had a tradition of gaol escapes – or attempts. Some ended in spectacular failure, such as the Manchester and Clerkenwell 'outrages' of the 1860s. Michael Collins became something of an escape expert for the republicans, helping with escapes from Cork gaol in 1918 and Strangeways in Manchester in 1919. When the republican leader Eamon de Valera was incarcerated in Lincoln with several associates, he was the obvious person to plot an escape.

With Irish republican history, a fair amount of myth gets mixed up with reality and this is true of the de Valera escape. Partly this was deliberate. In the aftermath of the escape, a republican in France, O'Kelly, told a version of the escape that owed little to the truth. In this

Eamon de Valera

version, the Irish had first considered a military assault on the prison, but then changed to an interest in an approach to the back gate through the exercise yard. The yard, outside the walls, was surrounded with barbed wire and guarded at night by soldiers, so not an easy route. Local girls were approached to divert the soldiers' attention, but none would help, so the activists sent to Dublin for 'two handsome young women, both highly cultivated university graduates'. Meanwhile, an Irishman rented a garden near the wall and sang Gaelic songs – which actually contained instructions to de Valera. As a result, de Valera made an impression of the key and threw it over to the 'gardener'; in due course the girls distracted the soldiers, the wire was cut, and the rest was history…except it wasn't. Almost all of O'Kelly's story was false; after all, he was a Sinn Fein officer, with an interest in ensuring that further escapes took place!

The reality was just as an exciting as O'Kelly's version. De Valera persuaded a fellow prisoner, Sean Milroy, to draw a postcard picture of a drunken man with a key, standing outside his hall door and saying, 'I can't get in.' On the other side, the man was shown a year later and in gaol, looking through a keyhole and saying 'I can't get out.' De Valera then got a third prisoner, Sean MacGarry, to send the postcard to an associate in Dublin.

The rather slack prison security arrangements failed to realise that this was anything other than a prisoner's humorous drawings. In fact both key and keyhole had been drawn carefully to the exact size and shape of the real ones in the prison – and the key was the master key. De Valera had managed this by taking advantage of Catholic church services.

De Valera helped to serve at Mass in the sacristy and had been able to get an opportunity to get hold of the Catholic Chaplain's prison master key. Whether he had been 'allowed' to do this might be a moot point. He had then gathered up the wax from candle stubs, warmed them by his own body heat, and taken an impression of the master key from which the drawing had been made.

However, there was a slight problem—the recipients of the drawing did not understand its significance! Four increasingly desperate attempts to 'drop the hint' were made by writing again in English, Irish and Latin until the penny dropped…

Back in Dublin, the drawing was then passed on to Gerry Boland who used it to make replica 'blank' keys, one of which he kept himself and two of which were sent to the prison inside a cake. These did not work, so another key had to be made. Messages between the prisoners and the 'escape committee' became increasingly fraught, to the extent that de Valera thought the prison authorities would notice and he considered dropping the scheme.

A third cake was baked and Boland actually delivered this—with the key—in person to Lincoln gaol having come over to England to help with the escape. Boland got the Chaplain to help with passing coded messages, which were to be relayed back out again from MacGarry via a visiting Manchester priest. The message 'I have applied for parole' meant that they would be ready to escape from the back gate at 6pm on 28 January, when the plan was to provide a ladder to get them over this wall; a message saying they had not applied for parole would indicate that the escape was not 'on'.

But plans went wrong again. The latest blank key had a slot in its centre which did not fit. So a fourth cake was baked and delivered with a toothless blank key and a file inside of it. On 31 January this was used by another republican inmate, the Mayor of Kilkenny, who happened to be a locksmith, to make a proper key.

On 3 February 1919 at 7.40pm, de Valera, with MacGarry and Milroy was able to use the key to open various doors and get themselves to a gate in the outer wall. The other side of this, Collins and Boland had gained access by cutting through barbed wire and were ready to 'spring' the escapees. Boland nearly gave the game away when he switched on his torch to give a signal and then could not switch it off again. Collins put a key into the lock, but it broke inside. For a few seconds the republicans were horror-struck – so near and yet so far. The alternative was to use a rope ladder to climb over the wall, but de Valera blanched at this.

Then de Valera pushed his own key into the lock and managed to push out the pieces of the broken key. In seconds they were out, but there were plenty of people around, including soldiers from a nearby military hospital, with assorted girlfriends. Boland wrapped the tall de Valera inside a fur coat, and held him tight as if in a romantic clutch. Thus disguised, they managed to escape to the nearby *Adam and Eve Inn* where they were picked up in a car and driven to Worksop. In the Nottinghamshire town they switched cars and continued to Manchester, though Collins went by train to London. According to O'Kelly's version, four other carloads of Irishmen were dispatched to 'career around the country roads of Lincoln' as a distraction.

De Valera was smuggled into Manchester, while the other two were hidden in Liverpool. On 20 February, Collins managed to get de Valera across the Irish Sea on the *Cambria,* and he was hidden in the Gate Lodge of the Archbishop of Dublin's house at Drumcondra. Later, and somewhat controversially, he made his escape to America.

The 'honey trap' was a favourite trick
(Illustration by Lee Mason)

Back in Lincoln, the escape was discovered a few hours later. Lincoln was festooned with handbills, offering £5 reward, but by then the republicans were well away. Inspectors Finn and Farewell led an investigation which exonerated as many people as possible by blaming staff shortages though it was also felt the convicts had enjoyed 'excessive liberty'. The rumours that prison guards had been diverted by 'ballad singing gardeners' and 'Sinn Fein sirens' with 'womanly graces' were discounted.

De Valera returned to Lincoln in 1950, when he was given permission by the authorities to visit the prison with Fenner Brockway, a fellow prisoner from 1919.

Author's Notes:
This is an historical story, and not a myth or legend in any way, except in the way that 'heroic' events tend to grow into legends in their own way. Some of the details change according to whose version you read, so in de Valera's version it was Boland who broke the key and also the number of cakes seems to vary! De Valera being disguised as a woman seems a detail too much for some authors of the tale.

I used press sources and also D Fitzpatrick, Harry Bolands's Irish Revolution; T Coogan, The Man who Made Ireland; F O'Donoghue (ed), IRA Jailbreaks; R T Dwyer, The Squad.

Chapter Fourteen

Murder of a King

The founders of Swineshead Abbey had chosen a spot in the Fens that they had hoped would be both safe from floodwaters and safe from too much outside disturbance. Though close enough to the Fenland road that some called the 'Washway' to give succour to travellers, they had hoped to be remote enough that the principle of hospitality did not conflict overmuch with spiritual contemplation.

Yet in October 1216 the monks looked out as a large and rather bedraggled group rode up towards their abbey, with the Royal Standard fluttering at their front. They were not surprised, because the King had already passed by on his way back from the siege at Lincoln to Lynn, passing through territory that was quite hostile to him in order to contract for new supplies at the Norfolk port.

The porter looked anxiously at the Abbot as they stood at the gate. 'There will be trouble,' said the porter, 'as he has lost his baggage in the mud and someone will have to pay.'

'There is always trouble with King John,' said the Abbot, and promptly wondered if it might be better to say nothing, but he continued anyway. 'It is always the poor who have to pay and, if not the poor, then the Church.'

Did King John really lose jewels in The Wash

The Abbot was reflecting on the years of turmoil that had accompanied Prince John and, latterly, King John. There had been the fight with the Church that had led to the Pope banning all church services in 1208 and even excommunicating the King. Then there was the constant warfare: with the French, the Scottish, with most of the barons and even his own relatives. At such times men were taken off to war, harvests did not get gathered in, winter stores were looted by passing armies. Yes, it was always the poor who suffered.

As John sat miserably on his downcast and weary horse, he mused that the year 1216 had also been a very difficult one for King John and an even worse one for many of his unfortunate subjects. Facing French invasion in the south, and rebellion in Lincolnshire and other points of the North, he had criss-crossed the nation with his soldiers, including a famous visit to Lincoln. Now his trip back from Lynn had gone disastrously wrong: a guide had tried to be too clever crossing one of the infernal muddy creeks and rivers; packhorses had got stuck and then rolled over. Bags and sacks of his goods had gone into the mud and the swirling brown waters. He'd shouted at men to go and fetch them, but some of them had gone down like the horses – and quite a few not come up. What had he lost? A lot of his supplies and perhaps even some his jewels; the rest he had bartered against future deliveries through the port of Lynn. Mud and water everywhere, yet he had never actually seen the sea.

Now he had to stay at some decrepit fenland monastery. The plan had been Sleaford – where the bishop had a castle – or a return to Lincoln, but now he had to stay in this ague-infested fen[3]. It wasn't surprising he felt feverish and that his stomach churned, and now he had to greet some obsequious monk who was standing at his gate trying not to look worried. As if an abbey that was named after pigs was going to have anything that the King might want to take! Except ale and wine, perhaps.

The King's mood went from bad to worse. He was forced to stay at the cursed abbey a couple of days while he waited for news of his missing goods, but none came and he concluded it was all lost. The monks were hardly ready to feed a king and probably hated him anyway; food was scarce and additional supplies curiously lacking for the time of year.

The final night of his stay King John finally lost his temper. The abbey's few monks hung around pitifully while he was at table, some of whom looked suspiciously well-fed to him, while the king looked at an overcooked duck, some eel, and a scrawny loaf.

---

[3] 'Ague' was 'marsh fever', similar to what we might recognise as malaria.

He picked up the loaf and glared at a monk. 'Tell me, monk,' said the king, 'just how much does a loaf like this cost?' The king had asked a good question, for the monk he spoke to had been responsible for organising the food and had taken some pleasure in setting before this infamous and ungodly monarch a loaf that would barely have graced a poor man's hovel.

'Well, sire,' squirmed the monk who now felt a little uncomfortable, 'a loaf like this costs barely a half penny around here.'

King John laughed. Normally people blamed him whenever the price of food went up: it was due to the King's taxes, or the King's wars, or the King buying up all the food for his soldiers. The King was a convenient excuse, it was even his fault if they forgot to sow their seed and no harvest grew!

'A halfpenny?' he said. 'Cheap. Well, maybe if I live another half year it will cost more. What would you say, twenty pence if King John still rules?'

These were bitter words, and they twisted in the soul of the uncomfortable monk. How could this evil monster laugh at such a thing, when it would bring starvation and death to thousands? Another year of constant war would ruin the land, another generation of children would never see adulthood.

But John was amused by his prophecy and repeated it to all the courtiers present, who laughed dutifully. Then he tore up the loaf and ate it piece by piece, chewing slowly and washing it down with ale as it was so hard. 'Twenty pence!' he laughed, 'and well worth it! Now, why is there so little ale to be had in this place?'

Seething, the monk left the hall to fetch more ale. If only, he thought, some of the rebellions against John had succeeded, yet the King lived and others died. Then a thought of such wickedness stole into his mind: that the King had been delivered into his hands through the food and drink he would taste at their abbey. King John was complaining of not feeling well. It would take only a little skill to worsen his illness and, since he had already complained, others might take the blame.

If John lived, others would die. Might the monk himself act so that others might live? Yet to kill a man was a mortal sin, and who knew what punishment might await the murderer of an anointed king – albeit one who had been excommunicated for a time? But it would be the simplest and easiest act, with an impact that would bring joy to thousands. John didn't even have a food-taster; perhaps that was another one who'd drowned in the marshland crossings.

The monk went to see the Abbot and explained the thought that had come to him. Was it of God or the Devil? Could killing a man ever be justified? The two men went to the chapel where they prayed to God, to St Oswald, to St Etheldreda and all the saints who had fought for goodness in times of darkness.

Then the monk said his confession and the Abbot spoke the words of the absolution. From then, they spoke no word to each other.

The village sign of Swineshead shows the King with a monk and a poisoned chalice

The monk took the largest wassail bowl from the store and went into the abbey garden, which was dank with the autumn rains. He found a toad sheltering in the reeds and put it into the cup, hiding it while he walked to the ale store. There he pricked both sides of the toad while it lay in the bowl, so that the infamous venom seeped into the silver vessel. Then he opened the best cask of ale, one that had been brought by boat from Flanders, and took it to the King.

King John had grown impatient. 'It took you a very long time to get this ale,' he said, 'Did you have to go to Lincoln for it?' But the king noticed that it was delivered in a strikingly beautiful silver wassail bowl, an old Saxon tradition. 'No sire,' said the monk, kneeling, 'but I have opened our best reserves of foreign ale as you seemed unhappy. I promise you, you will never have had such a draught as this, and I promise you'll never have a better one until the day you die. See, I also I have brought you it in this wassail bowl, a memorial of your Saxon ancestors.'

King John was pleased at this reference to his heritage, but he had not survived so long just by luck. 'Then if it is so good,' he said, 'you must drink it first and enjoy it. I will not have it said that I took the best from the mouths of monks.'

So, full of terror but outwardly calm, praying and seeking his peace with God, the monk drank deeply of the poisoned ale. Nothing happened, so the King took the ale and sipped – it was good. He drank some more.

'Now, if it please you, I will retire for the night,' said the monk and he slipped away, but he went straight to the abbey infirmary. There his stomach swelled and he writhed in agony until it split and he died. Five monks gathered around to sing prayers for his soul, in fear and trepidation for they knew not whether their friend's soul was journeying to Hell or Heaven.

King John was still in the hall, but he noticed the monks had all disappeared and he felt unwell. His mind was troubled as he ordered the table taken away and he rose to his feet, unsteady. He sent for the Abbot. 'Where is the monk who was serving me?' he demanded.

The Abbot was crestfallen. 'Sir, he has died,' muttered the Abbot, fearing for his own life.

John would have been apocalyptic with fury, but of a sudden he was overwhelmed by despair and heartache. There was nothing that could be done. He would live, or he would die, but he was weary of battle and killing and anger and misery. Already his stomach was swelling and he could feel pain starting to develop. He ordered the men to get ready for departure. If he were going to die, it would be in some place other than this.

At dawn King John left Swineshead. They carried him to Sleaford, where there was at least a doctor of sorts who let blood from him and muttered under his breath as if he knew what should be done. They tried to revive him with best peaches and cider, but he turned his head away and the servants ate and drank at his expense. Messages came from the barons, who wanted to surrender Dover to Louis of France, redoubling John's torment.

He pressed on towards Newark Castle, but the pain was so bad that he could not stay long on a horse and had to be carried in a most undignified manner. As he arrived, John knew that he might never go further and over the next few days the sickness inside him worsened. He sent for the Abbot of Croxton to confess his sins – it was a long discussion – and received the holy sacrament from him. Then he sent for the lawyers and clarified his will and the royal succession. He sent letters to all the barons and owners of castles, commanding them to show loyalty to Prince Henry. The Abbot of Croxton asked John where he wished to be buried and John said, 'I commit my soul to God and my body to St Ulstan.' And then he died.

That night all his servants and retainers fled, but they took with them anything that could be taken. They left not even enough cloth to cover the king's corpse, but he was taken to Worcester and buried near to St Wulfstan as he had asked.

Author's Notes:
The death of John is surrounded with myth and legend, with the only real certainty that he died at Newark having previously stopped at Sleaford. He had an accident on the route from Lynn to Swineshead, but whether he really lost all the crown jewels is a matter of debate. The claims of Swineshead as the place of his poisoning were recorded in Caxton's Chronicle of 1502 and popularised in the Gentleman's Magazine in 1785. This is not to say the claim was believed: Creasey's book on Sleaford dismisses it as reflecting 'the striking simplicity of the age in which it was written'. There is another Lincolnshire tradition in which John was poisoned at Sleaford by peaches and cider, or consumed too much and poisoned himself. More recent views have tended to him having contracted dysentery at Lynn, or possibly some problem caused by 'gluttony'.

Yet the Swineshead story is curiously gripping and worth preserving. There is a strong moral to it, for it raises the question of justifiable violence and the torment of the monk comes across powerfully even in the Caxton version. Questions over justifying violence against evil dictators became a major philosophical debate in the twentieth century, so there is something timeless about the monk's dilemma.

King John died at Newark Castle

Chapter Fifteen

King Canute and the Aegir

King Canute rode up the hill to the old warrior encampment on the hilltop above the hamlet of Gainsborough with some mixed feelings. His father, the great warrior King Sweyn, had seen both triumph and disaster here. Canute was familiar with the old stories that Sweyn had been killed by an apparition of Saint Edmund, but he also knew the rumours that not everything that had gone into Sweyn's banquet the night before had been quite what it should have been.

Canute himself had survived by playing all sides. He had embraced the Christian faith more fervently than his old father had done, but he had taken care to be a strong ruler who kept dangerously powerful nobles in their place. And he knew there were dangerous forces on the move: followers of the Old Religion resented their banishment and, it was said, plotted against him with well-placed friends. They said that the Danes, a sea-faring people, were foolish in the extreme to ignore the old gods such as the god of the sea, Aegir.

As Canute arrived at the old camp, he was surrounded with the usual flatterers. Most of these were minor nobles, anxious to cement their place on the ladder of power, but since his own power had increased they had become more numerous. Nor were they all to be trusted. Then there were the tensions between the English and the Danes, with the latter starting to argue that he was too tolerant of the former, who some saw as defeated weaklings. There again, there were some who saw his support for Christianity as pandering to the English rather than his own true people.

'Hail great king,' shouted one old warrior as Canute dismounted after his short ride. Though a Dane, he was glad to have both feet on solid land rather than standing on the timber of a ship or resting alongside horse flesh. Then a younger man, one of the aspirant nobles, shouted out, 'Hail Canute, ruler of the Danes and the English.' The young man looked pleased: he had outdone the old man.

'Hail, great king, soon to be ruler of Norway and Scotland,' yelled another, keen to win honour on the battlefield.

'Hail Canute, ruler of the winds, waves and tides,' shouted a fourth. Canute smiled, perhaps ironically, and looked through the gloom to see who had come out with this one. Yes, he thought, one of the weasels. But the weasel's call was a popular one, and soon boys and women were echoing his words around the firesides of the camp and the wooden hall.

That night, during the banquet, the boastful shouts continued. Canute was not sure if, in all cases, they were genuine or meant to rile him, but he noticed an old Christian priest was clearly not amused. Now, Canute was keen to show that he embraced the Christian faith, and so he beckoned the old priest over. The priest, who had learned that God was more reliable than the Danes, approached with some hesitancy.

'What do you say, old priest?' asked Canute. 'Do you think I could rule the waves and the tides – not forgetting the wind?'

The old priest took a moment or two to consider. 'No, your majesty, I do not.' The sound of breath being drawn could be heard around the hall and one or two swords shivered in their sheaths. 'Only God controls the winds, waves and tides.'

Suddenly, one of the younger men pushed his way forwards. 'Well, I say there has never been a greater king than Canute. The tides will surely follow his command!' Other young men shouted their agreement, all anxious to be seen to have greater faith in Canute than the next. But Canute turned to an old warrior, Ragnor, and asked for his opinion.

'Well,' said Ragnor, who was not a smooth speaker, 'I don't hold with these new religions. In my day, Aegir was the god of the sea and he ruled the waves and the tides. I recall how he would send his daughters to take a man to the depths. I would not like to argue with him.'

The young men sneered. What an old fool talking! When Ragnor was young, there had been no king as great as Canute. And so they began praising the king again.

'Enough!' shouted Canute. 'Tomorrow we will put it to the test. We will go down to the river when its waters are flooding back in from the sea, and I will see if by my command I can halt the tides. If I can then it proves I am the greatest king, if I cannot then some here today must have spoken falsely. Only the river itself can tell us.' Canute, of course, was playing a careful game but few here would have guessed that he had his own terrors, principally of Saint Edmund, who he feared might return and drive him to an early grave as had happened to his father.

Cnut, the warrior King

Well, that night some young men slept fitfully in their beds, recalling with unease the senseless flatteries they had uttered. What if the king failed to command the waters? Would they pay with their lives? In contrast, the old priest slept easily. He could see that Canute was not seriously challenging God. As for Ragnor, he slept well, but in his dreams the god Aegir rose up for one last sign before the old gods slipped into oblivion.

The next day was wet and windy, a bad spring day, not one for venturing out to sea. This was the first rain for days: it had been a cold and hard start to the year. Canute ordered a wooden throne to be carried down the hill to the river at low tide and placed on a muddy beach from which the water had only recently receded.

'Now,' he declared, 'we are ready for the test. If those who said so are right, then by my word the tides will not cease. Maybe the great waves will stop their inland race and return to the sea. If they do, then truly I am the greatest king. If they do not, then it is proved that no man has greater power than the Lord God himself, and those who said otherwise will be guilty of the worst type of blasphemy!' The young men shivered with fear: they knew the king was looking at them.

So Canute sat down, his royal feet resting in the mud, and spoke out. 'Oh, waves and tides, hear the word of Canute, King of Denmark and England, most powerful of earthly rulers. Cease your constant movement, hold back the tide, and come not further into this river.' Then he crossed his legs, settled down comfortably, and smiled at those around him.

Now, of course the river here was tidal of sorts but, being wider and shallower than it is today, its tidal range was less. As Canute sat, the water level barely changed until – very gradually – it started to creep back across the mud towards his feet. The young men shifted restlessly, their desperation growing with every small movement upwards of the water. As their desperation increased, they began to search for any excuse. Then one of them recalled a story the old priest himself had told them, about how Moses had grown tired and been helped by Aaron.

'Listen,' shouted the desperate young man, 'our king grows tired, just as Moses did. Let us help him!'

So the young men ran forward, all anxious to be the first to help. 'Stop fools,' shouted the old priest. 'Yes, cease this stupidity,' shouted Ragnar, 'and look down the river. See, here is your answer!'

All turned to look down the river. There, at a clear distance away, they could see a crest of water rolling up the river, turning ever over and over upon itself but gaining ground rapidly towards them. Women started to scream and boats moored on the river began to thrash at their moorings like turbulent horses keen to escape.

As the water approached so the level of the river rose all of a sudden – by the height of a child, or a woman or a man – depending on whose account you believed. Though the young men shouted and raced for the bank, Canute, Ragnar and the old priest stayed where they were.

The story of King Canute as illustrated in a child's history book

The water around them rose suddenly, engulfing the muddy bank on which they were placed, then quickly dropped away again leaving just the three soaking figures.

Canute was still in his seat, smiling. 'There you see,' he observed, 'no man is greater than the waves and the tides.'

'Praise to God,' cried the old priest, 'for He alone commands the oceans and the rivers!'

Ragnar stuck his sword into the ground and muttered, as much to himself as anyone else. 'Well, I say it was Aegir who rode past, making a last claim to his kingdom, and I don't care what anyone else happens to think.'

So they all went back to the camp and Canute went back to ruling England, Denmark and anywhere else that was available. The friends of the old priest won more converts, built more churches and secured the support of the monarchy. As to Ragnar, he faded away along with his old beliefs but he still managed a night or two of storytelling over a good drink and, in time, it was his version of the story that caught on and the strange wave on the river kept the name of Aegir. Which is why, if you go to Gainsborough today, you will still see all sorts of references to it, although not always spelt correctly.

Did Canute really try to stop the Aegir?

Author's Notes:
Well, I must admit that this story is almost pure invention on my part, but it contains elements that could be true. Having lived almost beside the Trent for a number of years, I have been struck by the lack of any known stories about the origins of the tidal bore called the Aegir, although it has many different spellings including the local bus company 'Eagre' perhaps. I also came across references to the famous story of Canute and the waves having occurred at Gainsborough, although other places, such as Southampton, might have better claims. I was interested in this pivotal time in religious history when the Danes chose to give up their Norse religion and embrace Christianity, yet the old faith lived on in the named features such as the Aegir itself. The 'ea' sound is also connected with water and we have many Lincolnshire placenames for places near to water that show this – such as 'Bardney' and also some rivers falsely called 'Eau' when they should be called 'Ea'.

As to spellings, I have seen Eager, Eagre and one old book says Hygre. The Aegir is really a tidal bore, caused by the forcing of inrushing water into a narrow channel. The Environment Agency website contains guidance on when and where to see it.

Chapter Sixteen

The Tap at the Window and the Knock at The Door

One day in 1678, Leasingham girl Alice Medcalfe stayed at home while her parents went to church. She happened to look out of the window and saw a man with flaxen hair standing in their yard. She did not know him and, being a brave girl, asked him his business.

'I have come to borrow a horse from your father,' he said, standing at the stable door. 'Well, I know nothing of it,' she said, 'so go to the church and meet him there. You cannot have it now.' The man turned and went away, with no complaint.

Her father said he knew nothing of the man, but nonetheless the next day both parents went to Sleaford market – and then the flaxen-haired man turned up again. He asked for a horse, and again she refused him, and then he turned towards Alice and began to use flattering words she did not like the tone of. So she shut the front door and bolted it, causing the stranger some anger. He began banging on it, and she became frightened. Just then there was a knock at the back door, and the friendly voice of a neighbour, into whose arms Alice almost jumped. Recovered, the two went into the yard but there was no sign of the stranger.

Alice was a cautious girl and she was reluctant to talk too much of what had happened for fear perhaps that people would think her mad, or a witch. But she told her mother and, through one thing or another, the two began to suspect that the village cobbler, Follet, had something to do with the strange appearances. Well, Follet was the only cobbler in the village and so one day he appeared at the yard to do his routine

Lesingham Church

work for them. Now it may be that Mrs Medcalfe had some doubts about employing him, but she had even stronger fears about what might happen if she sent him away, and so she set him on some tasks.

Follet insisted on talking – about Alice. 'I have some books,' he said, 'and from these I can get all sorts of knowledge that none others in Leasingham or hereabouts are party to. From these I can read all manner of serious warnings and this is one: that your daughter Alice will not see out the year.'

Mrs Medcalfe was horrified and turned him out. 'Be gone,' she cried, 'and let us see you never again!'

'You may never see me again,' he replied, 'but I can be certain you will think of me.'

And he was right, for soon Alice became very sick and for a while her mother despaired of her. They prayed that she would recover, and by Whitsun she was fine again.

By this stage the strange flaxen-haired visitor had almost been forgotten, and yet one day there he was in the yard again! He was at the door of the house this time, with a great club in his hand as if he intended to smash his way inside. Alice was now afraid, and shouted at him. This caused the stranger unexpected anger, and he flung down the club where it smashed into a pile of earthen milk pails. Then he stormed off, Alice bravely following him at a distance through the village until she lost sight of him. Curiously, when she got home she found none of the milk pails had been damaged.

Several times that week the stranger showed up in the yard, and every time Alice ran to get her father, but he never managed to set eyes upon the visitor. At the end of the week the stranger appeared again and told the girl he wanted to speak with her – but then declined to tell her what about. Then he showed Alice a knife. 'It is for you,' he said, but she in turn was not to be frightened and told him she would go and fetch the hangman for dealing with the likes of him. The next day he ran past the window with a knife but although her parents rushed out, they could not see him.

For several days in a row he appeared at the parlour window and seemed to have forced it open although it had not been opened for years. The knife was sometimes long and sometimes short, but always it bore the marks of blood and sometimes there was blood on the man's hands.

The Medcalfes employed a youth named Richard Cousins who was aged eighteen or so and he had naturally heard all about the flaxen-haired stranger. One day he was walking out near Roxholme when he saw a man who he thought must be the stranger. He hurried back to their house and fetched out William Medcalfe and his daughter, and soon Alice spied the stranger. Yet as soon as she pointed him out and her father gave chase, he seemed to change direction so that the father had to run around and round. He never could catch proper sight of the stranger.

Alice took to carrying a club with her and one evening was coming back from milking with it when she met the stranger in the lane. 'What are you doing with that?' he asked, though surely he knew.

'I have a good mind to lay it about your head,' she retorted, but the stranger just laughed and slipped away.

Time passed in this way until a day in July, when her parents were out and Alice was making her breakfast of frumenty using the freshest milk available. At this point Follet the cobbler appeared, and asked if there were any shoes to mend. Now, he was not a welcome visitor, and Alice was more afraid of him than of the other strange visitor. She knew her mother would turn him away, but feared his threats and so told him she thought they had some shoes but she would need to ask her mother. He went away, but when she returned to her frumenty she found the milk had turned to hard curd. Then the dish itself suddenly leapt up and danced upon the table, before throwing itself on the floor where the dog came and licked up the curd. The same day, out making hay, Alice turned her leg and went lame, a problem that lasted three months.

The next time the stranger turned up just as a wind blew her hat off, and it landed at her feet. Whether the strange visitor was getting bored by all this is not clear, but on his next appearance he spoke again. 'It is Follet who is sending me,' he said.

After this the Medcalfes started to have strange noises in their house at night. The doors of cupboards and rooms would be flung open and banged violently, whilst chairs and utensils were moved around. One day the barn doors were banged open and shut although there was no wind. On another occasion Alice said to her mother that Follet was the cause of this, and the very next second they saw him ride by on his way to Sir William York's house. Odd things kept happening, including one of Alice's petticoats disappearing and then re-appearing, while an apron vanished but returned full of holes! One night towards the end of summer the troubles got more personal: poor Alice's clothes were pulled off her, and her hair so twizzled and matted that it took her mother two hours to comb it and cut it.

Then there were appearances by a cat, which once got into the parlour and bruised and scratched her face. A note appeared wrapped round a stone, saying, 'I would have you go to…' She put it away to show her parents, but it vanished. Alice put out a clean shift on her bed to wear the next day, but it vanished overnight; she borrowed one from her mother, but this turned up torn and slashed before her own re-appeared.

Aside from some problems with a few of her father's possessions, this proved to be the end of Alice's troubles. Their servant Cousins left to work for Sir William York and we know no more of what happened to Alice.

The home of Sir William York was the finest house in the village of Leasingham, and Sir William one of the most important people around. But, as Member of Parliament, he was often away and this was the case in May 1679 when trouble came calling at his home.

It was late in the evening (which was about eight o' clock in those days) and Lady York was readying herself for bed when there came a knocking at the door. This was a great inconvenience, and so she listened for the sound of the servant opening the door and the voices which would tell her who came at such an hour. Yet she heard the door opened then, after a pause, closed again with no voices. Presently her maid came in.

'Please your ladyship,' the maid said, 'but Harold sent to say there was a bang at the door but no-one there.' Almost as soon as the words had left the maid's mouth there came another, rather urgent rapping at the door. Lady York went downstairs to find poor Harold, the butler, in a somewhat distressed state, for he had opened the door again and still found no-one there. This was odd, as the door opened into a yard which was surrounded by a wall ten feet high, with a locked door the other side.

Lady York and the few servants at home conferred urgently and they concluded that the knocking could only be a ruse by robbers to trick them into opening the door and letting the thieves in. So when the knocking came again, Harold put on his best and sternest voice and shouted through the closed door.

'We know your trick,' he said, 'and we won't let you in. In fact, even now Sir William is on his way back from Sleaford with armed men who will take you to the gallows.'

The knocking stopped, but only a few minutes later it started again, until the women of the house were quite terrified and Harold was trying to pretend that he was not. Then Lizzy, the scullery maid, remembered the hunting horn that Sir William kept and Harold was despatched to find it. He clambered to a top room in the house and blew it loudly from the windows, again and again. This worked. Within minutes all the folk of Leasingham were gathered outside to see what the fuss was, the folk inside shouted out their fears, but there was no-one at the door for them to arrest.

Over the next two or three nights the same thing happened and although the fear of robbers diminished, the confusion of the residents increased. Over this period some twenty different people heard the banging at the door, and though they looked out from upstairs windows, no-one saw a thing. They concluded that it must be some trick, but no-one could find string, stick or any other means of causing the knocking.

When Sir William returned from Parliament, they told him all about it, but he was inclined to dismiss it as the hysterical imaginings of women. Yet one night he was in bed, waiting for Lady York, who was undressing, when he heard the knocking himself. It continued for about a quarter of an hour and during this time Sir William repeated all the checks that the others had, opening the door, looking out of the window, checking for trickery. It stopped and started several times and continued almost to midnight, when it changed to a much more violent banging, almost as if someone were pounding their knee against the lower part of the door. Then it stopped.

In July Sir William and Lady York went away for a few days. One evening, the servants were sitting in the kitchen, awaiting their return, when they heard a noise as if the door to the cupboard under the stairs was banging and clapping. There was a short discussion as to who was to go out first, then they all rushed out together – and found the dining chairs all set in a pattern in the middle of the hall.

'Well, this wasn't done by robbers,' said Lizzie, and they all nodded wisely. But what could they do? So they put all the chairs back in the correct places. Yet as soon as they returned to the kitchen they heard banging and scraping again, and this time they found that the chairs had been moved to the passageway between the kitchen and the hall. It was almost as if someone wanted the house remodelled.

A few weeks later, in August, Sir William was getting ready for bed when he also heard a knocking at the door under the stairs, as if someone were banging it with a good thick stick. It stopped, and then restarted when he went back down. Then it stopped again. What could he do? So he went to bed.

Two weeks later, Sir William was in the closet by the hall when he again hard, violent knocking of the door under the stairs. It was normally kept locked, so he went to get the key (which took him a while to find) and then bravely opened it. The noise ceased, and there was nothing there to see. So Sir William gathered half a dozen of the family around him and they sat in the hall to wait – but no further sound occurred.

Now, Sir William was very suspicious about this and so he locked the door and put the key in his pocket before going up to bed. As soon as he was upstairs, the same noise started again and so he rushed back down – but everything was exactly as before. This happened four or five times that night, and every time he came back down to the door the knocking ceased.

Interest in apparitions increased during the late 1600s as shown in this drawing from a book of that era.

'It always does,' said Harold, 'except that first night. Whenever you get close, the knocking stops, but the first night we were able to shout at it through the door.'

A few nights later this pattern repeated itself, except this time the knocking was gentler, as if it were being made with a stick where the end had become broken or frayed. It continued until eleven o' clock.

By this stage Sir William was increasingly angry, his wife increasingly distressed and the servants were all threatening to leave their places and go elsewhere. He came up with a new plan – as soon as the knocking started, everyone would go into one room and stay together, Sir William thinking this would flush out the fact that one of them was responsible.

So as soon as it started they all went together, which pleased the servants mightily, since they were now very frightened. Sir William counted that everyone was in the room together – and then the knocking at the door under the stairs started again!

Now, the hall had a large room like a type of parlour which had never quite been finished and was unfurnished. In September, the noises suddenly transferred themselves to this location.

During the late 1600s writers such as Lincolnshire's Henry More became interested in the supernatural basing their work on Biblical examples.

At first it sounded as if a man were walking up and down in there, then as if he were running. Then it turned into an odd sound as if the man had bought a pair of stilts and was using them, and even banging on the ceiling above with them! But the same pattern – as soon as Sir William went to the scene, the noises stopped.

It was after this that things started to get very frightening. Sir William's elderly father lived in the house, as did his small children, and they found it increasingly difficult. The noises stopped following a pattern, and started occurring suddenly around the house at various points. He urged them all to move out, but as he insisted on staying they said they would stay too. They feared for Sir William's life if left on his own.

During this period, he called in some plumbers to help with a rainwater system. He wanted to divert water off the roof and into a cistern, which involved much banging of iron and leadwork. This was fine during the day, but when the plumbers went home in the evening it started again. Their work was being imitated! Carpenters also came in to do some work, and they chopped their wood in the yard before carrying it in; yet the noise of chopping continued outside even though they were all inside. Knocks started occurring at the outhouse doors: the wash house, the brew house and everywhere. But always the same – they stopped as soon as someone approached.

One of the worst attacks occurred when a visitor, Mr Brown, was staying in the house. On this occasion all the noises came, the whole repertoire.

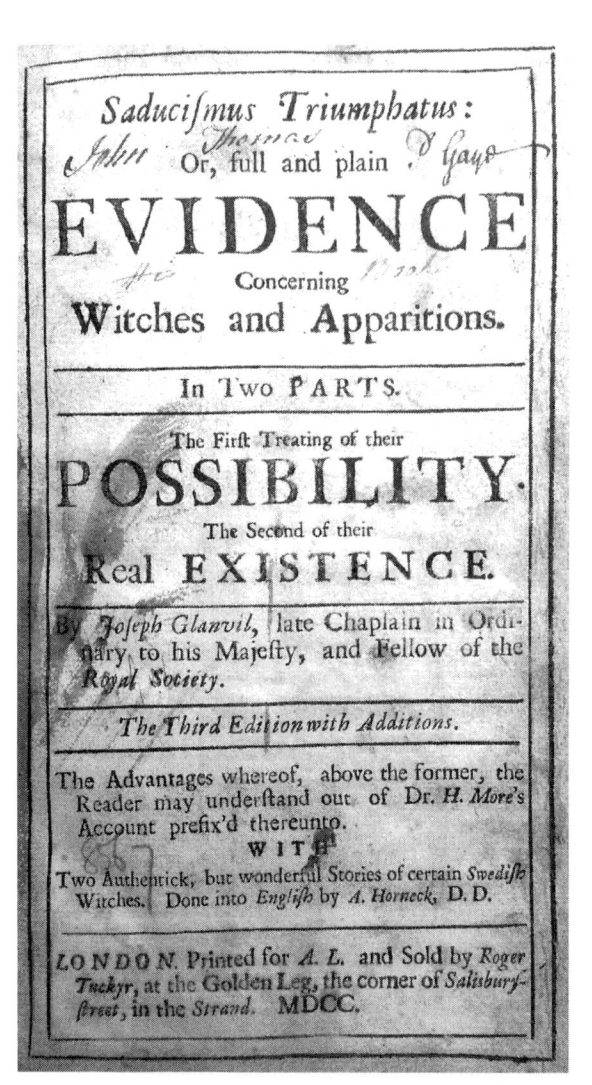

Henry More worked with the Royal Chaplain, Joseph Glanvil to collect stories of the supernatural

The doors, the windows, the unfurnished parlour, the ironwork and the new cistern were all banged. This occurred whilst the carpenters were all still in the house, and they were especially astonished at the ferocious banging at the front door, which sounded as if it were being pounded with heavy timbers. The carpenters expected it to give way at any moment, yet when they went outside to look there was not even a mark on the door. The noises continued, sometimes like the roof tiles were tumbling to the ground.

Sir William decided to fight with the only weapon he knew. When he heard a noise he marched towards it and spoke: 'In the name of God, who are you?' Each time he did this, the noise moved to a different place and so Sir William pursued it, candle in hand and God's name on his tongue.

Another night, there was an extraordinary commotion in the parlour, so he put his family safely in one room and went there with his candle and prayer. The noise ceased. He felt encouraged but still knew nothing. Reasoning that if God protected him when he carried a candle, He would still do so in the dark, he blew the candle out and waited. Sir William paced the room in the dark for fifteen minutes – silence. Then a tapping began on the outside of a window. He marched to the window, and shouted: 'In the name of God, what is the meaning of this?' The tapping stopped, but instead there came a violent banging on the sundial, some ten yards away in the garden, after which a series of bangings went around the house.

The same night Sir William took his family Bible and opened it, placing it in the space under the stairs where so much of the noise had come from. This made no difference, and the Bible appeared untouched. When the family huddled in one room there came a beating at the wainscot in another, just like military drummers this time, except as if made by a pair of hands on the wood.

Another night, the family were all at their evening prayers when there came another set of violent sounds. Chairs were moved, candles put out and snuff flung around. This time the candlestick had been moved to the passage between the kitchen and the hall.

This lasted the whole summer until it was October and time for Sir William to return to Parliament. He was worried about his family and Brown came to stay with them the night before his departure. This night there was only a gentle tapping and after that – nothing.

Author's Notes:
This story is taken from Dr Henry More's Continuation of Remarkable and True Stories of Apparitions and Witchcraft. More died in 1687 and I have used a version printed in 1700. I have put the two stories together, though in the book they are separate but successive chapters. More provides a commentary in which he links both stories to the cobbler and astrologer Follet, believing that such business as fortune-telling lets out all manner of spirits. I have told the story more or less as More does, adding only a few words of talk and the characters of the two servants at the York house. Nowhere in either story is there any indication of people seeking revenge on Follet and, for all the hauntings, no harm appears to have been done to anyone or anything, apart from Alice's illness and wounds from the cat.

The behaviour of individuals in the two stories is interesting. More must have seen some significance in the fact that Alice first encountered her problems when she should have been at church, but in the second story there is a sense that God is called in to protect against the Devil – yet no-one sends for the clergyman. And it is interesting that Cousins was in both houses.

Sir William York(e) was a real person and was MP for Boston at various times between 1679 and 1701. He was a reportedly Presbyterian, which might explain his choice of not calling in the parson.

Henry More knew Lincolnshire well: he was born at Grantham and was the clergyman for Ingoldsby. He wrote a number of theological books and, though some may now ridicule him for his beliefs in witchcraft and demons, he shared these interests with Isaac Newton, with whom he once discussed the Book of Revelation.